THE
RECRUITMENT
REVOLUTION

THE
RECRUITMENT
REVOLUTION

THE BLUEPRINT FOR HIGH-GROWTH HIRING

ROSIE SKINNER

TABLE OF CONTENTS

FOREWORD - HOW TO USE THIS BOOK AND WHO THIS BOOK IS FOR

"Great vision without great people is irrelevant." Jim Collins, 'Good to Great'.

This book is for entrepreneurs and business owners who have hit a wall in their recruitment, to the detriment of their business growth, and are serious about investing time and resources in making a change. Completing this book will provide you with a blueprint for creating a talent-planning strategy, and building a robust, repeatable recruitment process and a system that truly delivers.

Getting your recruitment strategy and organisational structure right is intricately linked to the success of a business. If it isn't right, or requires re-alignment, the business is unlikely to reach its goals.

In this book you will meet Dan, an entrepreneur running a successful scaling technology business but whose biggest headache is recruitment. It has become a barrier to growing his business, and occupies his every waking thought.

You'll also meet Anna, a recruitment expert who specialises in building recruitment strategy. She mentors Dan in how to transform his recruitment, thereby transforming his business in the process.

You can either follow their narrative along, or skip forward to the key takeaways, homework provided by Anna, or learn how Dan implemented Anna's advice from each section.

If you have the time and the inclination to follow the narrative as it goes along, you can recreate the blueprint that Anna and Dan put together, and which resulted in a successful turnaround for his recruitment. You will read not only Anna's specific advice, but also see how Dan interprets it and makes it work for his business. This will hopefully inspire you to make changes in yours! Reading the book in full will take more time, of course, but you will gain more insight from the experience.

If you only have the time to focus on the key takeaways, you'll still have your 'aha' moments, and will still be able to absorb the key points of the twelve steps to recruitment success. I also recommend looking at the homework Anna sets for Dan each week (Dan's Homework), and how Dan chooses to implement this advice (What Dan Did), as it may provide you with inspiration as to how her expertise can help your own business.

If you complete all of Dan's homework, and use the key takeaways at the end of each chapter to provide context, you will be well set up to make significant changes to your success in recruiting.

Dan has the help of a small team to support him in designing, delivering, and implementing the work set by Anna. If you are ready to make the same changes, establish whether there's a member of staff internally who can work alongside you, or investigate how you could outsource the work. There will be too many actions for a busy business owner to design and implement alone!

Dan also has the advantage of running a technology business, allowing him to expedite some areas of the process. If you don't have these resources in house, suggestions are made for manual options on relevant pieces of work, but again it's worth considering outsourcing where you don't already possess the internal capability to make significant change.

Finally, you can find informational blogs and templates to complement the core areas highlighted in this book over on our website: www.Mployable.co.uk

CHAPTER 1 - INTRODUCTION

"Sorry Dan - they made me an offer I can't refuse."

"And there's nothing we can offer to make you think otherwise?"

"I really am sorry. It's not been an easy decision, but I'm sticking where I am."

Dan said a hurried goodbye and ended the call. He resisted the urge to pound his forehead on his desk in frustration - even as the founder of the business, he chose to have a desk in the middle of the room, opposite his PA, Sarah, and next to the intern.

He exhaled deeply.

"Everything OK, Dan?" Sarah was looking up over her Mac screen at him.

Dan leaned around his. "Do you know what? That's the third person this month who's either accepted a job offer somewhere else, been counter-offered, had a change of heart, not shown up to an interview, whose cat has eaten their goldfish, or some other bullshit reason as to why they aren't interested in a job with us."

Sarah shrugged. "I really don't understand why we're struggling. We have an awesome office, a cool team and decent perks. You'd think people would be lining up at the door to work with us".

Dan looked straight at her, forced a smile and nodded with a sigh. "You'd think so. Maybe we're just going through a bad spell."

He got back to wading through the pile of CVs piled up in his inbox. It wasn't as simple as waiting and hoping: the whole growth of the business relied on making these hires. It relied on hiring more people, people with specialist skills and knowledge. People, who, at present, seemed about as easy to find as a four-leaf clover.

It was mid-morning and he had someone to meet. Pulling on his jacket he took the lift down to the ground floor and ducked across the street to his favourite coffee house, ruminating over the conversation he'd just had with Julia.

Did he sometimes say the wrong thing over email? Had the potential new recruit seen something she didn't like on the company Facebook page? Where had it all gone wrong? He'd worked so hard to build this company from scratch, late nights, early starts and a tense relationship with his girlfriend, Emily, were the price he'd had to pay for the early success the company was seeing now.

As soon as Dan had left Uni he knew the corporate world wasn't for him. Accepted onto a prestigious graduate training programme in the heart of Canary Wharf off the back of his first-class degree, Dan found out quickly that the 'small cog, big wheel' mentality wasn't where he wanted to be.

He'd studied Business and dreamed of starting his own. He had a revolutionary idea about an app that would change the face of online food shopping, and was determined to bring the idea to market. So he'd spent his evenings, weekends and early mornings developing and building the app, working around his graduate placement, getting ready to take his concept to market.

Emily had stuck by him since they met in the first year of Uni. Things had been fun back then, but as Dan had got sucked into creating and developing 'Trolley Deals UK' they had started to feel more disconnected than ever. Evenings spent with him hunched over his MacBook, working and responding to emails, with Emily nursing a glass of wine and attempting to tell him about her day. He wasn't really listening, but made appropriately interested noises. After almost seven years together, Dan knew Emily was desperate for a marriage proposal, but he was far too wedded to the business to think about that space for anyone else right now.

"The usual?" A chirpy barista broke his trail of thought.

"Please. Extra hot." Dan looked over to the table where Emily was already waiting for him. "And a double espresso, please."

As he waited for his coffee, his phone flashed. Nigel - one of the investors who helped Dan's business up and off the ground with a huge capital injection, but sometimes a bit too much day-to-day interference.

Dan plastered a smile on his face and answered it. "Nigel, great to hear from you - how's things?"

"Dan, my man! Fantastic as always. We changed our minds and chartered the plane down to St Tropez for the weekend after Paris, instead of coming straight home. A bit of sunshine does wonders for the soul!"

Dan cringed, but continued the pleasantries. 'It does indeed, sounds great.'

"And how did the interview with whatshername go? I know you were really looking forward to meeting her - we have been hiring for almost six months now, so it was about bloody time," Nigel chuckled.

Dan's heart sank. It was no secret that this hire was crucial to the growth of the company, but the specific skill-set was proving a big challenge to unearth.

"It didn't happen, Nigel. She cancelled right before; got a better offer from her current employer."

"Well, whatever it is, we'll match it - did you tell her that?" Nigel scoffed, confidently.

"I did tell her, yeah - but I don't think it's about the money. I think it's something else. I just can't understand what that something else *is*."

"Dan, it's always about money. Call her back, ask her price, and if you think she's worth it, we'll pay it".

Nigel was getting impatient now. His business reference was the financial sector in the 1980s, where he'd made his millions - very 'Wolf of Wall Street' - and the mere thought that someone couldn't be bought by the highest bidder was outrageous to him.

Dan was silently shaking his head, knowing that his over-enthusiastic investor was completely out of touch - but also knowing that he wouldn't let it drop.

"She definitely would be worth it, I know. Without this hire we can't continue to grow. If we don't start picking up pace with any of the recruitment, we're going to struggle. But the fact of the matter is, it isn't about money. We can match or exceed any offer in town, but still no-one is interested. It's something else - and I need to figure out what that is before the company begins to suffer as a result".

Nigel fell quiet, slightly stunned by the outburst from a usually placid Dan.

"OK Dan. Look, I believe in you and I believe in this business - that's why I invested. But if you won't take my advice on this, then it's something you need to work through on your own. Speak later." Three short beeps signalled the end of the call.

"Extra hot Americano with Oat Milk and a double espresso for . . . Dan?"

"Yep, that's me." He resolutely took their drinks to the small table already occupied by Emily.

"You look stressed," she noted.

"Nigel on the phone again. I appreciate all he's done for us and I know he took a big risk on me in the early days, but sometimes the interference really isn't helpful. It just adds to the list of pressures."

Emily gave him a knowing smile, "Recruitment again?"

Dan nodded. "Just before I left to meet you, the candidate we had booked in for interview today cancelled on us - said her current employer made her an offer she can't refuse."

Emily rolled her eyes in sympathy and reached out to touch his arm. "It will all be OK. These things have a way of working themselves out."

He smiled, grateful for how understanding she was about the place in his life that his business held.

"Thanks, Em, you always know the right thing to say. And you're right of course. But this recruitment problem is killing us. Without more people we can't keep up with some of the bigger fish in the market. In this industry if you can't keep up, you quickly become irrelevant."

His phone flashed again with the office number.

"So sorry Em, I'm waiting on an update on a project - mind if I take this?"

"Sure. I'm not going anywhere."

Dan mouthed a 'thank you', as he picked up the phone and walked towards the quiet of the open air outside.

Emily picked up her own phone and began mindlessly scrolling social media, grateful for the break in her day and some time with her boyfriend - albeit scattered with small interruptions - but she didn't mind. It was just the way it was. In fact, it was the way it had *always* been in their relationship, and she'd known that would be the case since the day they met.

A woman came and sat at the table across from her, and turned to face her.

"Excuse me, I'm so sorry to interrupt. Do you mind if I talk with you for a moment?"

She seemed friendly enough, she was smartly dressed, and it was a public busy café, so Emily felt safe to say yes. She was intrigued as to what this woman might want from her.

The woman reached out her hand.

"Anna Rose."

"Emily."

They shook hands.

"Nice to meet you, Emily." Anna smiled. "Look, I promise I'm not a complete oddball, but despite my best efforts to not eavesdrop I couldn't help but overhear the conversations your husband had on the phone and with you."

"Boyfriend actually, but yes - he's a bit stressed out at work at the moment. I'm sorry if he disturbed your coffee."

Anna laughed. "No, not at all. I was more thinking that I might be able to help."

Emily looked at her quizzically. "Oh, I see. In what way?"

Anna smoothly took out a business card from her business card holder and handed it to Emily:

Anna Rose, Talent Strategy & Recruitment

Emily read the card and thought for a moment. "You're a specialist in recruitment?"

"I guess you could say that."

Just at that moment, Dan came back. He looked at Emily, wondering who the woman sat opposite her could be. He didn't recognise her as one of Emily's friends.

Emily looked up at him, "All OK?"

Dan shrugged, "Sort of." He looked at Anna.

Emily jumped in, "Sorry - Dan, this is Anna. We've just met. I think you two might have something to talk about."

"Really?" He asked, glancing between the two of them, a bit confused.

Emily slid Anna's card over to Dan, and he read it with interest.

"As I said to Emily, I couldn't help but overhear your conversations about your recruitment challenges - and without making you think I'm some stalker who hangs out in coffee shops approaching strangers, I just wondered if I might be able to help?"

Dan smiled politely, "We don't work with recruitment agencies, I'm afraid. But I'll keep your card."

Anna laughed, "It's OK, I'm not from a recruitment agency. The way I work is about getting to the heart of the recruitment issues. Fixing the foundations, rather than papering over the cracks."

Dan was still unsure as to how to continue the conversation. "It's just the teething problems of growing a business, but we'll get over it".

"I know, I've seen it all before. Recruitment is one of the toughest challenges a growing business can face."

Dan nodded. Maybe he was being too judgemental about Anna. He could always search for more online about her later - and maybe she could help.

"I'd love to know more about your business, Dan." Anna was genuinely interested.

Emily gave him a nod of encouragement and settled back to listen.

He thought for a moment and decided to throw caution to the wind. He explained what the business was, and how it started. "We've gone from strength to strength over the last five years and our growth has been fast and upward. So fast and so upward, we rely on hiring the right people at the right time to keep on an even keel."

Dan paused to take a sip of his Americano. "In fact, recruitment has been one of the toughest issues we've faced over the last 18 months."

Anna nodded, knowingly. "Well the tech sector is challenging and competitive to hire within. Years ago, Google started offering sleep pods, state-of-the-art breakout areas, gourmet food and every other perk you could think of to entice the best talent, and now even the smaller companies have followed suit. In fact, most businesses are having to think outside the box to get themselves seen and heard by the best candidates. There's a new standard for hiring; it's a recruitment revolution".

Dan put his cup down and looked straight at her, with interest now. "I've never thought of it like that before - tell me more?"

Anna smiled. "Yes, that's part of the problem: most businesses don't even know it exists. They still recruit like we did in the '90s - some even placing adverts in the local newspapers, crossing their fingers that that will do the job, and then being surprised that no-one suitable applies."

Dan chuckled. "OK, well we aren't *that* bad - but I am wondering if we can be better. In fact, we need to be better. The success of our next update relies on bringing in two new software engineers with specific skill sets. Without that internal capability we're really going to struggle."

"Well, that's probably where we can start. Talk me through what you're doing now."

"You know, the usual. We put up an advert online and as soon as anyone applies who looks like they could be a fit, we call them in for an interview. We're quick, we don't hang about, we're a good team and we have nice offices. I just don't know where it's going wrong. We're really trying."

Anna took a moment to reflect.

"What's the consequence of not making those hires?"

"Honestly, in terms of revenue? Potentially millions. In terms of our team, they'll be putting in late shifts, early shifts and weekend shifts to try and create solutions to work around the problems. I guess I'll be sleeping at the office for the next few weeks - and Emily probably won't be all that happy." Dan half smiled, a feeble attempt at keeping the conversation light.

"No I won't, you're right!" Emily was only half joking.

Anna slowly put her drink back on the table and sat back in her chair.

"Dan, I can help you. But here's the thing: you've got to want to work *with* me on this. I don't have a silver bullet solution; there's no such thing. But I can show you a tried and tested method for successful and consistent hiring. It relies on buy-in and collaboration from you and your team. It takes time and hard work, but what you get in return, is results."

Emily held her breath during the silence. It might all be too good to be true but solving this recruitment issue would be the breakthrough Dan needed professionally - and for them personally.

Dan thought for a moment, considering her proposal. "I'll make the time. This is so important to me." He looked at Emily and could see how hopeful she seemed. "So. What's next?"

"We're going to work through a blueprint for hiring and talent-planning. It's a method I can show you, and you can take away to implement consistently, ensuring you see the right results every time. I call this method the 'twelve steps to hiring success'. It's the revolution of recruitment, and it will give you a fool proof method to stick your head above the parapet and become an employer of choice, appealing to your ideal candidates."

Dan was finally convinced. "Sounds great. Where do I sign up?"

Anna laughed. "I'll tell you what: if you're happy to meet here once a week, same time, same place for the next three months,

THE RECRUITMENT REVOLUTION

I'll coach you through the method. I like what you're doing, and you can buy the drinks. But you must show up, and you must do the homework in between us meeting - sound fair?"

Dan didn't have to think for too long. "Anna - you've got yourself a deal. Thank you."

The three of them clinked their cups together. It had been quite the unexpected morning.

"Oh, and Dan, here's your first piece of homework: dig out your organisation chart for me, and any material surrounding your organisational structure and bring it to our next meeting."

Dan nodded, and he and Emily said their goodbyes to Anna, as she left.

Emily turned to him, eyes shining. "Well. How about that?"

Dan sat back into his chair, taking a moment to reflect on what had just happened, Anna's business card still laid out in front of him.

"Look, I'm always a bit sceptical about these things, but if she can do what she says she can do, then it will change everything for us. Let's see how it goes."

Emily looked at the clock on the wall. "I've got to dash, but let's talk about it again later. I just can't believe that just happened. It must be fate."

Dan laughed at her enthusiasm, and couldn't help but feel swept up in it.

If Anna really could help him, it would transform the business and probably change his life in the process. Now, if only he could remember where that organisation chart was saved.

CHAPTER 2

As Dan walked back to the office, he felt a new sense of excitement wash over him. Truth be told, the recent struggles with hiring people had been starting to wear him down. Wondering why nobody wanted to work for his company, his 'baby' as he saw it, was soul destroying - not to mention time consuming.

Trolley Deals UK was located on the fifth floor of a beautifully renovated factory building, now housing a number of serviced offices. They occupied the whole fifth floor and were almost at capacity. In fact, that was the only saving grace of the recent recruitment struggles: at least an office move wasn't imminent.

Dan sat back at his desk. Sarah still tapping away while eating a vegan salad from the local deli.

"Good walk? You look a bit less stressed," she asked between forkfuls of salad.

"I think I found the breakthrough I was looking for," Dan replied. "Sarah, do you know where the organisation chart is saved? Or anything on our organisational structure?"

Sarah looked thoughtful for a minute. "I don't think it's been touched for a couple of years, but I'm guessing the HR file - or maybe admin? I'll have a look for you."

"Great. Forward it to me when you find it?"

"Got it, I'll send it straight over."

"Thanks."

The document popped up in Dan's email inbox, and he opened it immediately, not too sure what it would show. Sarah was right: it had been years since he'd thought about it.

He could see his team from three years ago, documented in a 'mind map' style format, with dotted lines and straight lines running between the names on the page. He had been keen when he first started the business to ensure that he ran a flat, non-hierarchical structure, so it was a simple document. His whole business on a 2D page.

"I couldn't see anything on 'structure' - this was all we had," Sarah called over the partition.

Dan took a minute to assess what was in front of him. Sure, there were a few names missing and some people had since left the business, but it still kind of worked, didn't it?

He pulled out Anna's business card and forwarded the doc to her, with a subject line of 'homework done - A* student yet?'

Anna responded almost immediately. 'Thanks Dan. We've got a lot of work to do. See you next week, mine's a latte.'

Dan had been expecting a slightly more positive response for delivering the document she'd asked for so quickly, and found himself slightly disappointed. But he soon forgot about it and the day passed quickly in a blur of meetings, phone calls and project work.

He left leave work at a sensible hour, with the sense that change was on the horizon. He lived just a short walk from the office block, a walk that took him along the river path, and as the sun began to set on a pleasant spring day he felt a brief sense of calm wash over him. A calm he hadn't felt for a long time.

As he put the key in the lock, he knew Emily had likely already been home for an hour or so but wouldn't be expecting him yet. As he walked through to the kitchen she clocked him, and a huge smile spread across her face.

"What are you doing home so early? Fire at the office?" She smiled wryly.

Dan's face broke into a grin. "No, no fire at the office - I just wanted to make some time for us. What do you fancy for dinner?"

"Actually, I stopped at the shop on the way home and grabbed one of those meal deal things, so you can just bung it in the oven.

They spent the rest of the evening chatting and eating. They reminisced about university days, the crazy nights out, the long summer days and the lack of responsibility back then. They talked about Emily's job and Dan's business and then the chance meeting with Anna earlier that day.

"She was really interesting Dan. If she can help you get to the bottom of your hiring problems, it could mean huge things for the business. World domination!" Emily finished with a final flourish - possibly a little giddy after her second glass.

Dan laughed. "Well it would certainly start to put us back on an even footing."

Overall, it was one of the best evenings they had spent together that year.

The rest of the week passed in a merry-go-round of meetings, deadlines, and projects and all too soon it was time for Dan's first meeting with Anna. He left the office with a bounce in his step. "The usual today?" asked the barista, recognising him.

"Please, and a latte?"

"Both extra hot?"

"Sure, thanks."

He took the coffees over to a table and took a seat.

Exactly on the hour, Anna swept through the door with a certain presence that caused a few of the other customers to look and see who'd arrived. She moved her sunglasses onto her head and joined Dan, shaking his hand and taking a seat opposite him.

"Latte, as requested."

"Thank you," she smiled, taking a sip. "Wow, bloody hot though."

"Oh, sorry, I always get drinks extra hot. I never know when I'll find the time to drink them. So it's kind of a beverage insurance policy," Dan shrugged.

Anna smiled, "I get it! Thank you. So, I've seen your organisation chart. Tell me, upon reflection, what do you think of it?"

Dan reflected for a moment. "Honestly, when I first dug it out I didn't think it was that bad. It makes sense to me - I can see all the people in the business and who they report to, without any of that hierarchical BS. Its colour-coded by department, and yes, there are a few people missing and a few people that have left now - but overall, I think it's fine."

Anna looked at him, "OK - ready for your first session?"

"Never been more ready."

STEP 1 - THE POWER OF THE ORGANISATIONAL STRUCTURE

"See, Dan, this is where it all starts. The organisational structure. It's a role map for your business. It is the foundations upon which you base your hiring decisions, and actually has nothing whatsoever to do with the actual people in your team."

She sipped her drink and continued.

"Traditionally, the organisation chart has been related to the people, and the organisational structure related to the roles and responsibilities. This division works well in large and corporate organisations, but the amount of paperwork and confusion it can create becomes inefficient in a smaller business. What I propose is a hybrid: an organisation chart that focuses on the roles and responsibilities."

Dan looked confused. "I'm not sure I follow."

"The people in your business are performing roles that have been created by the growth of your business. Your organisation structure and chart hybrid will allow you to map out the roles that you need to find the right people for."

"I'm still not quite with you."

"OK, let's talk about someone on your team."

Dan thinks for a few seconds. "Sarah, my PA."

"Great, so you've given Sarah the title of PA, and I can see on the chart here that that is exactly what she's marked down as. Tell me a bit about what Sarah does at Trolley Deals UK?"

"Well all the obvious stuff: booking travel, arranging my diary, special projects, administrative work - everything you'd expect a PA to do, really," Dan shrugged.

"You say 'administrative work' - can you expand on that?"

"Erm, well she looks after some of the day-to-day HR stuff, contracts for new starters, makes sure the stationary cupboard is topped up and all the office ordering is done. She takes care of the company social media and deals with any PR enquiries. Oh, and she's brilliant at making sure we never run out of milk. Super important - caffeine keeps us going!"

"So, what you've just told me is that Sarah is PA to the Director, the Operations Manager, the Office Manager, the HR Assistant, the Admin Assistant and the Marketing Assistant?"

Dan looked at her, a realisation dawning on him.

"The *people* are inconsequential. It's the roles that matter. And people in your business, particularly in a growing business like yours, will likely wear many hats. While it seems insignificant now, as you grow it will become essential."

Dan was nodding, but not totally clear. "Why is it so essential to understand the roles?"

"Because that's how you start to establish the gaps, the overspill and the stretch. As you grow, if you understand explicitly the hats everyone within the business wears, you will see where resource is best allocated, based on *value*. This then allows you to establish when you need to hire, promote, train, or outsource. This, Dan, is the very foundations of your talent plan and recruitment strategy. Without this, you're fumbling in the dark."

"I think I'm getting the hang of this. Let's go back to Sarah, so all of those things you said she actually is - and I'd never thought of it like this - is a Marketing Assistant?"

"Exactly Dan, that's the point. And tell me, is her time spent as a Marketing Assistant of *value* to the business? Is it the right role for her experience and skill set?"

"Well, she's rather good at the company social media; she had to be, to get the role. Many hats, and all that. But it's likely not where her skill-set is best deployed. There's probably someone else in the team now who could take on that responsibility, freeing up her time to work more on projects with me, which I could really use the support on."

"Exactly. That's the purpose of this exercise: are the right people in the right seats on your bus? Because your business is going to keep evolving, and skill-sets that got you here might not be the right skill-sets for five years' time. But you need to understand what your business looks like from a role perspective, not a people perspective, to be able to figure that out."

Dan thought for a moment, as Anna took a long sip of her latte.

She put it back on the table and continued.

"So, for your second piece of homework I'm going to ask you to do three things."

DAN'S HOMEWORK STEP 1

1. Redraft your organisation chart using this method, as the business is today. Think about the structure and the chart, to create your hybrid.

2. Create an organisation chart, again using this method, for how you predict the business will look in five years' time. And finally,

3. Create an organisation chart, still using this method, for your business when it is completed. What the final line-up will look like, how you see the team looking when the business is 'finished' by you."

Dan was furiously scribbling all this down in his notebook.

"OK, got it. That really makes sense. I suppose in this context, the names of the team are inconsequential because people need to be fluid, it's the roles that are fixed."

"Correct," smiled Anna.

"What's your opinion on organisational structures being hierarchical or flat?" Dan asked.

Anna thought for a moment. "It makes planning simpler if you use traditional structure and reporting lines, but I understand why some businesses don't like to promote a hierarchy. It's received a bad reputation from some corporate environments over the years, but the truth of the matter is that if you have fixed line managers who have direct reports, no matter how you dress it up or play it down, you have a hierarchy."

Dan continued writing notes in his pad, as Anna carried on talking. "There are companies that don't work to a traditional hierarchy system and are extremely successful. They work on a 'project lead' or 'revolving lead' basis, where each member of each team acts as the manager at some point, dictated by their expertise and the expertise required by the project. The best-known method is called 'Holacracy'. But even in this case you'll still see a CEO, or an overarching leadership in some form. Ultimately, every business has a structure of sorts. Creating an organisational structure using the Holacracy method, or something similar, adds a depth of complexity to the picture. It's about what is *right* for the business."

Dan tapped his pencil, deep in thought. "I need to take some time to digest and get some clarity on what this looks like for us, but this already feels like progress."

He flicked up his sleeve to look at his watch. "Anna, I've got to shoot, but thank you - this has been really insightful. Same time next week?"

"Same time next week," she confirmed.

Anna watched Dan leave the café, finished her latte, collected her belongings and headed to her next meeting.

Later that day, after an afternoon of long meetings, heated discussions, and stuffy rooms, Dan finally found some breathing space to think about the conversation with Anna that morning. He had an hour plotted in his diary to work on projects and decided that this was the most pressing.

WHAT DAN DID - STEP 1

- He started by making a list of all the roles in the business, everything he could possibly think of that his team do, regardless of whether it matched their formal job title or whether there was even anyone currently in the business hired to perform that role.

- He then sketched all the roles in the business into a chart with boxes and lines, marking where that role sat within the structure of the business. After some careful thought he made the decision to stick with a tradition reporting structure. He'd done some research into Holacracy, and although certainly interesting, he wasn't sure that the business was mature enough to cope with that level of disruption just yet, but he didn't completely dismiss it as a future consideration.

- Next, he wrote a list containing the names of each of his team members.

- Finally, he began to populate the boxes in his diagram with the names of his team, the boxes already titled with each of the roles in the business. He was surprised to see how stretched certain members of the team had become.

This snapshot of his business showed him exactly where his team were positioned, and even from a glance he could identify those who weren't being utilised effectively, or who clearly had too much on their plate.

And the person who appeared in the highest number of boxes? Him. That had to change. To grow this business he decided he needed to start to hire new recruits into the entry-level roles, currently occupied in some cases by himself and senior members of staff, to free them up to work on the higher level, strategic and business-critical work.

Once Dan had this clearer picture of what he was currently working with, he then repeated the exercise for five years' time, as per Anna's instruction, adding in the roles that he projected the business would need in order to cope with growth, already seeing the gaps they would need to train and recruit for over the coming years.

He finally repeated the exercise one more time for his vision of the business when finished.

This is where he found the method really came into its own: it's particularly challenging to predict whether people will stay in a business for another five years, or possibly more. Focusing on the *people* element of the document had held him back from such forward thinking. Now, by allowing himself to think only about the *roles*, he could temporarily disassociate from the people and consider only the structure of the business.

Dan leaned back in his chair and exhaled the breath he had been holding. Basically. He needed to hire even more people than he had first thought.

Shit.

5 Key Takeaways from Step 1

1. Organisational structure forms the foundations of the talent planning, organisational growth and the people plan.

2. Organisation charts provide clarity when they focus on the roles in the business, not specific members of staff.

3. Build the structure with the roles in the business first, only adding the appropriate names afterwards.

4. People will probably have more than one role within the business - some more than five. This is completely normal and workable as long as no team member is under-performing or stretched beyond capacity, and all employees are in a role that allows them to work to their full and true potential.

5. The purpose of the organisation chart and structure is to understand where the gaps, stretch and resources are currently deployed across the business. It is NOT a hierarchical snapshot of the company. It is worth researching other methods of organisational structure such as Holacracy, to decide what's the right fit for your business. But sometimes the traditional way is the simplest way to start, with a view to iterating as you grow.

CHAPTER 3

Dan had a restless night's sleep. He knew the recruitment issue needed addressing, but it felt like pulling the end of a ball of wool and not knowing where the end was or the chaos it might cause.

To implement the new organisation structure would mean big changes: promotions, sideways moves, growth and recruitment - more recruitment than he originally anticipated. It would mean him and his team truly stepping up to the next level.

He needed time to think this through before their next meeting. Anna had said that this was the foundation of the process, and as such it needed to be right. With a small team in the mix, a loyal team that worked hard for him, he had one shot at communicating and delivering the restructure before people might become unsettled and start looking elsewhere.

Emily walked into the kitchen as he was making himself a smoothie.

"You're up early," he said, wondering if he'd kept her awake with his worrying.

"You were tossing and turning all night, so I figured as I was awake anyway I'd cut my losses and get up to see you before work."

Dan paused for a minute, conscious of time. If he left now, he could have a 'golden hour' in the office all to himself to think. He put down his bag.

"I've got time - let's have breakfast together."

Emily smiled. "I think it's just about sunny enough on the terrace."

"Perfect."

They made their way out onto the neat little terrace. Dan sat back and let the very first glimpse of sunshine warm his face, sipping his smoothie.

"So, how's the work with Anna going?" Emily asked as she started to eat her breakfast.

Dan laughed. "Honestly, it's a can of worms but it's going to work. If I'm being honest with myself, it's work I should have been doing years ago, back when the business started. It's going to mean some changes with the team, but for the first time in a while I feel clearer about how we are structuring things."

"Well, that's great - so what happens now?"

"That's the reason neither of us slept particularly well last night," Dan looked at her apologetically. "We need to look at an internal restructure and we need to recruit more people. More people than I initially thought."

Emily thought for a moment. "You gotta do what you gotta do, right? You've done an incredible job to grow this business as far as you have, and as long as you position it right with the team I have no doubt they'll continue to support you, and understand the decisions you have to make to keep growing."

"You're right. The moves I'm proposing will benefit the team I've already got. It's a promotion for many of them, and a sideways but strategic move for others. Workplace upward mobility." Dan drained his glass, picked up his bag and kissed Emily on the forehead. "I've got to get to the office, but I'll see you tonight?"

"Sure," Emily said squinting at the sun. "Have a great day."

"You too."

Dan was first one through the doors of the office, despite the pause for breakfast. He was glad. An open-plan workspace had seemed like a great idea when they first moved in, but sometimes he really needed the space to think.

He got to his desk and pulled out his notes and the rough copies of the organisation charts, and took a good look at his design. On his laptop, he started pulling together his notes for a project proposal-style document. He highlighted the key areas for growth, redeployment of internal resource, and finally the roles within the business that he was still doing, but probably shouldn't be. He then outlined the possible outcomes for each move, indicated a ballpark cost for additional salaries, training, systems and a modest administrative recruitment budget, putting his faith in the method that Anna would show him and assuming they wouldn't require third party support and the subsequent hefty fees.

By this point a few members of the team had begun filing in, reusable coffee cups in hand, starting the process of booting up computers and greeting one another.

"Morning Dan, nice evening?" Sarah asked, placing her bag and coffee cup on the desk.

"Great thanks - you?"

"Not much, just ate some food with my flatmate and watched some series or other," she replied, eyes fixed on the screen as it came to life.

"Have you got 10 minutes now? I'm working on a project and I'd like to brief you. I need support on pulling a document and presentations together."

"Yes, of course, I'm pretty sure the meeting room's free until 9."

"Great, I'll follow you," They both picked up notebook and pens and made their way to the glass-walled meeting room.

Dan proceeded to give Sarah a potted overview of his meeting with Anna, and the outcome of the last session.

Sarah sat and listened with interest.

"OK, that sounds interesting. It's a big project, but it sounds like this woman knows what she's talking about. Do you even know who she is, though?"

Dan thought about it. "She works in hiring strategy and consultancy, but I don't really know much more than that if I'm being honest," he said, making a mental note to ask more questions the next time he saw her. "What I'd really like from you, if possible, is some support in creating a proposal and overview document to allow me some headspace to review the situation from a different perspective. Do you think you can come up with something today?"

Sarah mentally flicked through her to-do list.

"Yes, I might need to juggle one or two meetings and request a couple of hours of 'do not disturb' time, but if you can send me your notes I'll do what I can."

"Great, thank you," Dan smiled, "I've also got the first drafts of the proposed organisational charts - could you also please draft those up using the workflow software?"

"Sure thing, but can I make a couple of points?"

"Of course."

"Well the first, most obvious question when anyone talks about restructuring a business is about the security of our jobs. I'm telling you now, if anyone in the team gets wind of this, everyone will become nervous - and that's the last thing we want, because I'm assuming no-one will actually lose their jobs in this?"

"Correct."

"So, we're just going to need to be very careful about how we communicate and execute this."

"Absolutely. My task now is to establish the plan for the first steps and how we move this forward. This project is completely confidential until I say otherwise."

"OK, understood." Sarah exhaled, a little relieved. "Second point is resource. How are we going to manage hiring all these new roles? We can barely manage the ones we've got. Are we just trusting that Anna will help us through all of this?"

Dan nodded. "Look, I completely understand why you're nervous about this, and I'll be honest - so am I. But Anna or no Anna, I've realised that we need to step things up a level for this business to achieve its full ambitions - and we can't do that without more people, and without refocusing the people we've got. Stick with me - let's see how this plays out."

"OK," she nodded.

"We done here?" Dan asked, making a move to leave.

"Yep, I'll have the docs with you by the end of the day."

"Awesome - thank you." He pushed through the door and they both headed back to their respective desks.

Sarah delivered exactly as Dan expected, and looking through the documents he felt a rush of excitement in the pit of his stomach; something he hadn't felt since the early days of Trolley Deals UK.

Dan spent the rest of the week refining, tweaking and adding to the plans with Sarah's help, and on the day of his next meeting with Anna he was all ready and in position in the coffee shop when she arrived, exactly on the hour as usual.

"Dan, how has your week been?" she asked as she removed her sunglasses, placed her bag on the floor and settled into her chair.

"Interesting," said Dan with a slight smile. "The homework you gave me last week - the organisation charts - has been a catalyst for a big internal resource project. It was a method I'd never considered before, but it's going to change the way we work."

Anna looked at him, interested. "Tell me more."

"Well, the key thing I identified when I removed the individual people from the bigger picture was how underutilised some key members of our team actually are. How they're being bogged down with administrative work that doesn't correlate to either their skill-set or their pay grade."

He took a sip of his drink.

Anna nodded intently, "Go on".

"The number of roles within the organisation is much bigger than I anticipated, and when I went to put the team back into those roles it was like putting back together a jigsaw puzzle - but my first attempt to go back to the current status quo didn't fit. I realised very quickly that some of the team should be occupying different roles."

"Great. So what does that mean for the business?"

"Honestly, a restructure and some additional hires - although the majority will be at a more entry level than first anticipated."

"Wow, more hiring. And what's the plan for that?" Anna said wryly.

"Well", Dan put his coffee cup back on the table, "I was hoping that's where you come in, actually."

"Let's see what you've got." Anna sat forward, poised to look through the paperwork he was laying out in front of them.

"Our team are brilliant, and we need to keep hold of who we've got at all costs. But by taking the time to think about what they are good at and where they could add value, it opens up a whole tier of the business, predominantly admin and operations. We could hire, outsource or automate at a much lower annual cost, than continuing to hire into the senior roles we're currently really struggling to find."

"Dan, I think this is brilliant. Really well done. It also takes us nicely into today's session: talent planning, recruitment forecasting and, overall, the importance of timing."

Step 2 - Talent Planning and Recruitment Binoculars.

"The most important thing to understand about talent planning is that it's purpose is to be relentlessly focused on supporting the company's overarching business strategy: they must work in perfect harmony for both to succeed. Your organisational structure is also intricately linked to the operations of the business. If neither are right, or if they require re-alignment, the business is unlikely to reach its goals.

Now we've got a picture of the business from a capability requirement perspective, i.e. who we need to hire, and we've got a picture of your current team from an internal resource perspective, we can start to pull this together into a talent strategy."

Dan was listening intently.

"Looking at everything you've mapped out; you have clearly identified areas for change:

- You've found the gaps, the stretch, and the square pegs in round holes.

- You've identified opportunities for succession planning with your grass roots strategy and identification of internal training needs.

- You've made a strong choice to move people up into roles that stretch their capabilities, and free up entry-level or administrative roles.

How do you think the team will feel about all this?"

Dan thought for a moment. "Once they understand that their jobs are safe, and that this isn't a restructure in the sense of redundancy or job loss, they will be more comfortable. In fact, I think most of them will be excited about the chance to increase their capability and expand into more specialist areas of the business. There will still need to be some specialist capabilities brought into the business, but on the whole, we need to focus on who we've got and build around them."

"Couldn't agree with you more." Anna nodded. "It's often simpler to find candidates to fulfil roles at a lower skill or specialism level. It also creates a nice narrative from an employer branding perspective: hiring at entry level and growing your own talent from *within* the business - your own grassroots strategy.

This will work well for you."

"Excellent. So where do we go from here?"

"First things first: the people you want to move up in the business can't do that without your new team members in place, already trained and poised to take over the day-to-day work. You can never underestimate the administrative or operational functions - sometimes mistakenly viewed as 'low value' by organisations because they have low tangible output, but make no mistake: without admin, order and support the business will quickly fall into chaos."

"That makes total sense."

"On that basis, while I suggest that you speak with your team internally to update them on the changes and ensure everyone will be happy with their new role and the changes that will bring for them, we already need to start building a plan and a timeline to bring these new hires in, which aligns with your timeframes for up-skilling and training your current team."

"Isn't it just a case of advertising and hiring the right people when we find them?" Dan suggested, keen to get started on this new phase of the business.

"Only if you want a stream of people entering the business in quick succession, ready to be trained, ready to shadow. If you have the capacity and resource to on-board multiple individuals at the same time, not to mention run the recruitment processes and make time for interviews, while ensuring that it doesn't impact the running of the business, then it's something we can consider."

Dan raised his eyebrows.

"But," Anna continued, "if you don't have the systems and processes already documented and in place for this to happen smoothly, I suggest we create a recruitment forecast and a timeline."

RECRUITMENT FORECASTING

"A forecast?" Dan asked, trying to keep up with all the new terminology and processes.

"A recruitment forecast, yes. Think of it like a cashflow forecast or a sales forecast, but for your recruitment. It's a mix of facts and best-guessing, based on growth predictions, the current information you have on the comings-and-goings of team members and trends you've witnessed over the years."

Dan listened carefully, thinking it all through as she talked.

"For example, you might know that someone in your business is retiring, going on maternity leave or maybe even you've heard on the grapevine that someone isn't happy and they're looking elsewhere. Or maybe you're aware of a large new customer coming on board, and to service that customer you need to bring in new staff in operations, and that in turn means a new HR assistant to look after all those new staff, and so on and so forth."

Anna paused for a sip of coffee.

"It's all about trying to mitigate surprise when it comes to hiring. The examples I've outlined are rarely a surprise; they usually come with at least a few months' warning, and yes, of course things can change, as they must in a growing business. But just as with your cashflow forecast, you must update, assess and move on. The reason many businesses are on the back foot with hiring is that they don't plan. They know the changes that are happening in the business, but don't consider the impact that will have on recruitment. They are then surprised it takes so long to hire great people and end up in constant recruitment fire-fighting mode."

Dan felt his first big 'Aha' moment. "That's exactly what we've always done! I never even considered there could be a way of thinking ahead in recruitment to avoid the panic."

"Exactly. And don't beat yourself up about it; you aren't alone in this. Very few businesses of your size and growing at the rate you are, have any idea this is even a concept. But it's crucial to get this right, to review it regularly and stick to it wherever appropriate."

"This is going to be so helpful. How do we start turning this into a plan?"

Anna started to walk him through the key steps of creating a recruitment forecast, by first asking him about the 'at risk' or potential 'flight risk' team members: anyone who might be leaving the business either temporarily or permanently in the next six months. Dan told Anna about Emma in accounts, who was five months pregnant, but they hadn't even begun to start the searches for her cover. He told her about Justin, one of his top development guys, for whom he'd paid a princely sum through a headhunting agency. Justin had been in the business for a little over two years and Dan had overheard the end of his last telephone conversation, which sounded suspiciously like a conversation with a recruitment consultant.

"That's the problem with headhunting." Anna said. "If you find someone good, you'll be taking on a highly sought-after employee who knows their worth in the recruitment marketplace. Sometimes you might get lucky and they stay, but usually, especially in your industry, they'll generally have a shelf life of 2-3 years maximum. You'll have paid a hefty sum in recruitment agency fees, which for a business like yours, isn't sustainable."

"Absolutely right," said Dan, wincing at the memory of the bill from the recruitment agency. It was more than some of his employees make in a year. At the time it had seemed worth it, but he hadn't appreciated that the bill from the agency didn't buy Justin's loyalty forever.

Anna looked at him straight. "This is where we can start to work through the variables. By getting the processes in place, you won't be left in a Justin situation again because you'll have your recruitment binoculars on."

"Recruitment binoculars - I like that! We should make more of an effort to see what coming and let it influence our hiring."

Anna smiled. "You've really got this. OK, so tell me about how the business is growing - what else have you been working on?"

Dan told her about the areas where the business was growing most, the additional resources they would require to meet their ambitions in the next six months based on the internal movement, and where the gaps would open.

"And then there's the work we currently outsource,' he continued. 'As we've grown, there have been elements of the business where it made sense to outsource, or at least outsource parts of, and pick up any slack in-house."

"Outsourcing can be valuable to a small business, but as you grow you need to be smart about what becomes more cost effective to pull back in. We need to add the outsourced elements back into the equation, and establish the cost of this outsourcing, including partially outsourced areas plus the time you take working on it in-house. *Then* we can look at the cost of bringing it in-house," Anna concluded.

Together they listed out all outsourced elements, and Dan was surprised to find that a niche piece of development they currently outsourced was costing them a small fortune on every iteration. In addition, as it was one of his top developers checking the work, it was also costing him his time.

"Realistically Dan, looking at the numbers, it's going to be much more efficient and cost-effective to either outright hire for this role, or up-skill one of your team members."

"Agreed." Dan exhaled, slightly shocked by the numbers.

"The next thing to consider, is not just the roles you've outlined as part of your growth, but the ripple effect that has on the whole business; the impact this growth has on other areas of the company."

"Right." Dan looked at her quizzically.

"For example, if you're telling me that in the next six months you'll be taking on ten new team members in areas of the business from sales and marketing through to admin and delivery, and you have no in-house HR capacity, that's not going to work. Those are the honest conversations you need to be having around your recruitment forecast. I see growing businesses that try to scrimp on the business operations functions in favour of sales and delivery, but all that happens is the best members of their delivery team spend precious time answering the phones and co-ordinating holiday calendars for their team, not doing what they're paid for. That's when you get frustrated, because your top team aren't delivering the results you pay them for."

"I think that's where we are now, and why we need to elevate the current team away from admin, and focus on delivery by bringing in a business admin and operations team to sit around them. It'll make a huge difference."

"Awesome," Anna smiled. "So, let's build that forecast."

Anna and Dan mapped out a six-month timeline, with a

list of the roles they predicted the business would need to hire within that timeframe, allowing for natural turnover of staff and the growth of the business. This list was referred back to the organisational structures Dan had already drawn up to ensure cohesion, and to check that these proposed hires really would help move the business towards them.

"Dan, to recap, what I'd like you to do for me before we meet again is:

Dan's Homework - Step 2

1. Look at what's going to be happening in the business over the next six months and plot these hires into a timeline, in order of priority. I'd advise being cautious of hiring too many people all at one time; wherever possible, spread it out over the six-month time frame.

2. Take into consideration that your specialist roles could take anywhere from three to six months to hire, including notice periods, and that your admin or business ops roles will likely take two to three months from posting the role to when they start. Plot appropriately.

3. Run it past someone in the business who's 'on the ground'. Sometimes as the Director you can be a bit removed from the day-to-day operations, so have your plan sense-checked for a healthy dose of realism.

Is that doable before next week?"

"I can make the time." Dan said, excited to get going.

"Brilliant. You know where I am if you need to call me or send anything over via email." She glanced at her phone. "Got to go, but have a great week, and I'll see you next time."

Anna left at pace, leaving Dan alone with his thoughts and

THE RECRUITMENT REVOLUTION

the numerous pieces of paper that lay in front of him. He realised that once again he had forgotten to bring up the subject of her background, to get to know more about her. He was so consumed in their discussions about his business it had completely slipped his mind. It would have to be a conversation for next time.

He went back to the office and immediately asked Sarah to block out any afternoon she could in the next week in their diaries, to build the hiring timeline. He needed an extra pair of eyes and ears on this project, and a healthy dose of realism. Sarah was much closer to the everyday goings-on of the business and would soon tell him if his ideas were completely unrealistic.

He filled Sarah in on the meeting with Anna, where they were at in terms of the plans, what the new structure looked like, what the future hiring plans looked like and the task ahead.

"I will need your support on this one. It's a big project and I want to make sure I'm not getting carried away."

"Of course, Dan, it feels like it's coming together, and Anna's point about outsourcing is completely right. We're outsourcing in areas we could actually bring in-house by hiring or upskilling."

"Or hiring juniors and apprentices, to start to build a grassroots strategy and future-proof the growth of the business." Dan countered.

"Brilliant. This is exciting, Dan. Right, date is in the diary for us to get together Friday PM. I've cleared your schedule and I've got no plans that evening, so I can stay as late as you need me. If that's all good, I'm off out to grab some lunch - want anything?"

"I'm good, thanks. And Sarah, thank you. I really appreciate your positivity and support on this project."

She gave him a thumbs-up and disappeared off in search of lunch.

Friday quickly rolled around and at 1pm on the dot Sarah and Dan were holed up in the meeting room with Dan and Anna's notes spread out in front of them.

WHAT DAN DID - STEP 2

"This is where we need to get to: these are the hires we identified by pulling apart the skills-gaps in the business, based on the new structure. I still need to discuss this with the team, to ensure we've got buy-in before we move forward."

"OK, great."

"There are also a few areas we can build up, and we can buy some simple software to reduce those that are just weighing the team down, like HR. Currently it's managed by line managers and supported by a professional, legal phone-line service if we need it. But it's messy and chaotic. Loads of spreadsheets about holiday and sickness that aren't always up to date, and each manager runs to their own system. Based on our needs, we're going to bring in some HR software that allows the team to self-manage their holiday and sickness, and all managers can oversee it in one place. It can also store details on performance reviews and all other aspects of people and HR. We'll engage with an outsourced HR consultant to support us with any issues that crop up and to review our paperwork, in line with our growth plans. Longer term, we might consider hiring a HR Manager, but this system works for the foreseeable."

"Perfect, sounds sensible to me. One of the gripes from the managers is always the HR element of the role. They appreciate that it comes with the territory of being a manager, but I think they'll love the idea of automating and streamlining the process." Sarah said.

"OK, so next we're looking at the hires themselves. As we've discussed before, if the team is happy with the restructure then we're predominantly looking at hiring at an administrative and operational level. There are one or two specialist roles in the mix, in places where I don't think we already have anyone who could easily be upskilled to cover these gaps, but that's fine. We'll build them into the early stages of the plan on the basis that they may take us a while to find."

"Right, let's try and pull this together into a plan then."

Sarah was already excited by the challenge. They spent the rest of the afternoon debating the importance of various roles, the capacity of the team to execute the hires, whether it should be outsourced or automated, and finally at 8pm they had a plan. It written in pencil so it could be rubbed out, changed, or altered, but to Dan and Sarah it was a masterpiece.

"I think we've cracked it," Dan said, triumphantly.

"I'll be interested to hear what Anna thinks, but I'm really happy with it," Sarah said, putting her pencil down at last.

Dan looked her. "Thank you so much for your help, especially late on a Friday night. Go home and I'll see you Monday. Feel free to come in a bit later if you want, make up for this evening."

"Cool, thanks Dan, much appreciated." She began gathering her bags. "Did you find out more about Anna, by the way?"

"You know what, it completely slipped my mind again - I was so engrossed in putting this plan together that I didn't even think," Dan replied, honestly. "I'm sure it will come up at some point."

"I'm sure it will - have a great weekend."

"You too," Dan waved, as she left.

He let out a huge sigh of relief and reviewed the document

they had created. Then he texted Emily to say he was on the way home, gathered his things, setting the office alarm and locking up the building as he exited into the last of the evening sunshine.

5 KEY TAKEAWAYS FROM STEP 2

1. Planning and timing are the cornerstones of building a successful, proactive recruitment strategy.

2. Recruitment plans and forecasts must have flexibility built in. Much like a cash-flow forecast it's a mix of facts, best guesses and goals - your predictions will change, and the plan must have the capacity to change with it.

3. It is rarely a surprise that you need to hire. Make a note to regularly pick up your 'recruitment binoculars' to understand the changes happening in your business.

4. Outsourcing, automation and grass roots hiring, or 'succession planning' are a key part of your talent planning and recruitment strategy. Use each element appropriately to future-proof your business.

5. Specialist or senior roles can sometimes take up to six or even twelve months to fill, by the time you've accounted for time to hire and notice periods. Fact. Don't let it keep surprising you. Keep your recruitment binoculars on and stay out of firefighting mode.

CHAPTER 4

Dan arrived in the office on Monday morning, invigorated and excited for the week ahead. With the organisation structure, talent plan and recruitment forecasting coming together, his focus for the week was a one-to-one meeting with every member of the team to discuss this restructure, reassure them that their jobs were safe and hopefully excite them with the possibilities of the new roles within the business, along with the training and up-skilling opportunities.

While planning for a meeting with one of the more senior members of the team, an email arrived from Anna.

I'm heading to a global recruitment conference in a few months' time - here's the link. It would be great for you; you should book a ticket.

A

Dan, intrigued, clicked on the link. The conference was in New York, and it looked interesting: interactive workshops, networking with business owners and keynotes from some of the top names in recruitment from around the world. The headline speaker looked remarkably familiar: he recognised the long, dark hair and friendly face staring out at the screen straight at him. The blurb read:

Anna Rose, global hiring strategy expert and renowned consultant in successfully scaling up businesses through people resource. Former hiring manager for some of the biggest names in tech and digital, Anna is an expert at driving business growth through strategic hiring and talent planning, creating her own successful blueprint 'The twelve-step hiring method' that she successfully delivers to business owners around the world.

I suppose that answers that then, considered Dan, thinking back to his conversation with Sarah on Friday night, as he continued to look at the details of the conference. It looked rather good and it would be cool to see Anna in action. He responded:

I'll ask Sarah to investigate the logistics for me, but it certainly looks interesting. I'm sure I recognise the headline speaker...

D

A response came within seconds:

See you in a few days' time.

A

Dan forwarded the email to Sarah.

Sarah, can you investigate the possibility of me attending - my availability, travel arrangements etc. Thanks.

D

Dan checked his watch. Almost time to begin the staff meetings.

The week flew by, and overall the team was excited by the changes he was proposing. Most were looking forward to a new challenge and didn't mind the short-term disruption, for a business that served them all better in the longer term. He had one resignation from someone he knew had been unhappy for a while anyway, so following an open conversation they'd decided it was in their mutual interests to part company. Aside from that, the whole team was on board.

Before Dan knew it he was sitting in the coffee shop again, waiting for Anna with the drinks in front of him. At dead on the hour as always, she swept through the shop, headed straight towards him and sat opposite him, taking a grateful sip of her drink.

"Dan, great to see you again. You're looking well. So, tell me about your week? How did it all go?"

"It's been great. It took hours of my time and focus to get it right, but we've cracked it and it's exactly what the business needs to move forward. Sarah and I put this together on Friday," he finished, pulling out a one-page document with the key high-level points of the project.

Anna glanced at his review, making her way through the bullet points, focusing on the numbers and dates.

"This looks great Dan. Some of the dates are a bit ambitious - how do you feel about that?"

"I thought you might say that," he smiled. "Sarah and I decided it would help keep pushing things forward to make the changes - but there is some flexibility built into the background."

Anna looked at him with a half-smile. "I appreciate your commitment Dan, but just be careful. If you push yourself too hard and this project becomes unrealistic, your focus will wane and you'll become disappointed. My suggestion would be that if you are set on pushing yourselves this hard, trial it for a month and see if it works for you. Don't be afraid to adjust the timeframes if you've miscalculated."

"Understood. I'd like to *aim* for the dates though, but yes, we'll trial it and adjust if necessary."

"Great. How did the rest of the team take the news?"

"Overall, pretty well. We've had one resignation, but it was a mutual decision to part company. He hasn't been happy for a while and in all honesty, I think his role is one of the ones that's been impacted most during this process. Now I think about it, there's possibly some correlation there, so perhaps the truth is that role was never right for him in the first place?"

"I'd say almost definitely," confirmed Anna.

"Overall, it's been met with a lot of positivity and support." Dan took a sip of his coffee. "What happens next? I'm assuming we actually start hiring people?"

STEP 3 - TREAT YOUR RECRUITMENT LIKE MARKETING -EMPLOYER BRANDING

"Well, yes and no. Yes, in the sense that we will start the process for some roles swiftly, especially as you've identified a couple of roles that you need to start the hiring process for within a month. In fact, to keep up, we're going to need to run these sessions to build your strategy and process concurrently with the actual hiring. But the next thing we need to think about is a complete mind-set shift into thinking about your recruitment in the same way as you think about your marketing."

"Hmm, interesting. And how do we do that?"

"I assume your marketing team have built your brand around defining a target audience, and developing messaging that will appeal to that demographic?"

"Yep, it's been one of our USP's, the way we've narrowed it down and cornered our market. It'san integral part of our success."

"Great, so that's the first step with your recruitment marketing.

- Who is your ideal candidate?

- Where might we find them?

- How will we get in front of them?

- What messaging will appeal to them?

At this stage, skills, qualifications and experience are irrelevant. We'll drill down into those on a role-by-role basis, in much the same way as you would look at your individual customers, or customers for specific products or service lines in your marketing. What we need to do now is build a picture of your ideal candidate. What do they look like to you?"

"You want to talk about that now?"

"Let's get some key headlines down and you can complete the picture as some homework for the week."

"For us, it's generally people who are passionate about technology, and the opportunities it brings. Whether you work in admin or tech, you've got to be passionate about what we do. Secondly, it's positivity. Growing a business is hard enough without people moaning or complaining to each other. I look for people who want to work in an entrepreneurial, growing business and understand that that means hard work, pulling your weight, occasional late nights and heaps of accountability. I need people who come from a small, growing business background. We've hired from corporates or some of the big businesses previously, and the culture shift is huge. It's never really worked out for us."

"You're not alone in that," Anna said, comfortingly. "Often candidates themselves don't appreciate the mind-set shift from a corporate or big business into a smaller one. But identifying that now will pay off in the long run. But we're getting clearer, which is the first step. Next thing: where might we *find* these people?"

Dan considered the question. "I suppose the first obvious answer is with our competitors or businesses we respect."

"Yep, great start. Another action point:

- Research how your competitors, or businesses you respect, are currently hiring.

- Where are they advertising?

- What does their online presence look like?

- How are they delivering their messaging?"

She paused to change track. "But where else might we find them?"

"Well, I suppose Universities or Colleges that are renowned for producing the best in our industry?"

He looked at Anna questioningly.

"Yep, absolutely. We can come at that from two different angles. The first is to consider educational providers from a grass roots angle:

- First, consider how many training contracts, graduate programmes or apprenticeships you can offer and support realistically.

- Then you reach out to the training providers and engage with the department heads and the education recruitment teams.

- Finally, you engage. You could extend an invitation to an event, or attend their careers fairs - there's plenty one can do to engage, which allow you to grab their attention over and above your competitors."

"Sounds great - all of that we can do. What's the second angle?"

"Alumni. Although you'll be unlikely to find anyone who's ten years post-degree and still in touch with their old university, many of the big education providers have networks we can tap into, or bulletins that are still followed by graduates for a few years after leaving."

She paused.

"Also, if you have universities or training providers in mind that are preferential, we can proactively search for those people via online platforms and CV databases, using the name of the education provider as the key word or key phrase."

"I'd never thought of that."

Anna smiled. "You get the idea. Once you're clear on what that ideal candidate looks like, think about where you might find that candidate, and ways to get in front of them. Next, we need to think about messaging and tone of voice that appeals to the people we're trying to target."

Dan thought for a moment. "Going back to what we said about looking for people who've worked in small businesses and are excited by the challenges that brings, is there something in *that,* as a selling point?"

"I'd say so. You'd be surprised at the amount of people out there who are interested in entrepreneurial, high growth businesses with great teams, healthy autonomy and a cool product. In fact, many candidates I speak with today value those attributes over huge salaries, fancy titles and big offices. The key drivers for candidates in today's workplace are:

- Genuine work/life balance.

- Flexible working.

- Short working weeks, for example a 4-day week.

- Remote working options.

- Purpose. This could be either personal or social purpose, but something meaningful to the candidate, and makes them believe in what they do.

- Mastery. Training, and the opportunity to improve.

- Autonomy. A 'no micromanagement' culture.

Dan considered her points. "So if I've got this right, we need to define what's important to the target candidate we've identified, and package that up in a message that's clear, honest, relevant to us and aligned with our values, as well as theirs ?"

"Nailed it. Effectively you are creating a brand for your recruitment. An industry term for it is 'Employer Branding'." She checked her phone. "I've got to dash in a minute, but just to recap, ready for next week I'd like you to:

DAN'S HOMEWORK - STEP 3

1. Build a clear picture of your ideal candidate. Think about who they are, where we would find them, who they currently work for. What do they do in their spare time? Likes and dislikes? Which websites do they visit? What social media platforms do they use? Anything you can think of that will drill down into this character and build a clear picture.

2. Establish where you will find them. Bear in mind that the purpose will be to either contact them directly, lead them

to us, or passively advertise to them. So again, take some time to build a picture as to what this looks like. Some of your research in step one will probably provide answers here. Ensure the information is aligned.

3. Create a tone of voice and clear messaging that aligns with your values and mission, but appeals to your target candidate as well."

"Happy and clear?" Anna asked.

"Branding our employment: crystal clear. Thanks Anna. Oh wait, before you disappear - the recruitment conference in New York looks great, thanks for thinking of me. Sarah's scheduled it in, so I'm looking forward to it."

"I think it'd be good for you. There will be other business owners and recruitment industry insiders. People to network with, share pains and wins - you'd take a lot away from it. Plus, the line-up for speakers is stellar." She winked. 'Next week?"

"See you next week." Dan confirmed, and she made for the door.

WHAT DAN DID - STEP 3

Dan headed back to the office and made a beeline for Alex, their Head of Marketing.

"Alex, can I ask Sarah to put an hour in our diaries later this week? I've got a project I'm working on, and I'd really value your input."

"Yeah, no problem. My calendar is completely up to date, so just get Sarah to whizz something over. Sounds interesting," he replied.

"It's around the restructure and hiring project we discussed earlier this week."

"Well, I'll be really interested to hear more."

"You certainly will. I look forward to it!" Dan called over his shoulder as he headed back to his desk.

When he asked Sarah about booking in that hour for him and Alex, he added, 'I think it will be a good idea for you to join us too, so please check it works with your schedule.'

"No problem."

When he and Alex met two days later Dan was excited to hear what he might think of the concept of recruitment as marketing.

Alex was already up to speed at a high level on the project, as he'd had a meeting with Dan to discuss what his role looked like following the forthcoming restructure. Dan now filled in some of the gaps on a 'need to know' basis, explaining that the next step was to create a brand for their recruitment.

"An Employer Brand," he finished, looking to Alex for a reaction.

Alex contemplated for a minute. "Makes complete sense, it's something I know a lot of the global corporates do on a massive scale - I didn't realise it had filtered down as far as us, but now I can see it really does. We're struggling to hire, yet we have so much cool stuff happening here. Maybe that has been part of our issue with recruiting; we're just not shouting loud enough about all the great stuff we do, so we're getting lost amongst all the other tech companies in town?"

"I think you've highlighted the key issue perfectly," Dan said. "How do you feel about working with me and Sarah to develop this brand?"

Alex exhaled. "We have a massive backlog around the last

campaign, but if you can feed me some vision and ideas I'll pull together the internal resource to get things moving over the next few weeks."

"Great." Dan gathered his papers together. "Look I've got to shoot, but thank you for agreeing to support this project Alex, and Sarah - there are some notes on my desk about this from my meeting with Anna. Can you look and see what else you can add, based on the conversations we've had?"

"Sure thing."

"Thanks guys," he said, and made his way to the main office door.

Leaving the office before 5pm was rarely heard of for Dan and he noticed a few heads glancing his way, curious as to what had caused him to be the first one out for the day.

He got home before Emily that evening and relished the thought of having an hour to himself in the quiet of their house to think. He took a cold drink out of the fridge and sat at the kitchen table, then got out his notebook and created a mind map around who his perfect candidate was. He thought about everything, even down to:

· What they might wear

· Where they might shop

· Their values core values and motivators

· The things that were important to them as an individual

He then also thought about:

· The values he held both personally and within the business

· The things that had been important in building their team

- The people he had hired who hadn't worked out.

He could see it clearly and knew exactly the type of people his business was looking to hire. Next, he needed to work out how he would find them. A project for Sarah, he thought, taking out his phone and capturing pictures of his mind maps and notes. He sent them to Sarah and Alex, attached to an email:

Thanks for this afternoon, here are my thoughts on who we are looking for and what we are trying to build. Interested in your thoughts.

Actions:

Sarah - please can you research and create a report as to where we will find these people, including your thoughts on my notes and pass to Alex.

Alex - please subsequently build a strategy as to how we get in front of them, and what we say.

Have a great evening.

D.

Just as he was finishing he heard a key in the lock and Emily walked in, smiling as she clocked him at the kitchen table.

"Home early again? You seem to be making this a habit," she raised her eyebrow at him, putting her bags in the cupboard. "Good day?"

"Actually, it's been a really good day; I came home early for a change of scenery to work through some ideas. I can see clearly now what we need to hire for and who we should target. I think it was there all along but because I'd never articulated it, there's been a disconnect whenever we hired in the past. That's why I was finding it so frustrating."

"Makes sense - so when is your next session with Anna to talk it through?"

"I've still got a few days to get this right. I've sent my ideas through to Sarah to add to and research, and to Alex to get his thinking cap on about what the messaging looks like, so hopefully I'll have something concrete to take to Anna."

"Great - it's really coming together! Shall we eat?"

"Sure, I'm starving after all that thinking!" They spent the evening chatting through his ideas, and then moved on to everyday life things, Emily's job and what the future looked like once Trolley Deals UK was settled and Dan could step away a bit.

"The thing is though Em, if I can get this hiring right, get the right people in the right places in the business, I won't be needed there anywhere near as much as I am now. I can then take a real step back and focus more on the strategic direction of the business rather than the constant firefighting."

"And maybe we can get on with our lives? Think about getting married? Starting a family?" She looked at him hopefully.

Dan paused and carefully considered his answer. "I hope so. But you know I need the business to be secure and settled before I can focus my attention on anything else - I've never pretended otherwise. But if I can make this work, if I can bring in the extra team members and up-skill the team I've got so they can become better managers, and improving the structure, then I can focus more on my life, our life, outside of the business."

Emily looked at her empty plate. "I do understand, and you know I support you. But I hope you also know that I won't wait forever. I have every faith in you - but I really hope you can pull this off."

"I will, don't worry. This is going to work. I'll make sure of it."

She smiled.

"Right, I'm off to bed," Dan announced. "Another busy day in the office tomorrow, and I need to be on top form."

"'Night," called Emily over her shoulder.

The next day, as usual, Dan was first in the office and saw that Sarah had left a document on his desk.

"She must have been in the office late again last night," he murmured out loud, thinking she was really owed some extra time off to show his appreciation for her dedication.

He read through, reviewing how she had referenced ideas, facts, figures and statistics on where to find the new target demographic. Some items were less tangible, particularly around core values, and for these Sarah had provided well-constructed thoughts and ideas.

For others, including the personal likes, dislikes and leisure activities of this target candidate, she'd been able to give him some high-level figures from various social media platforms about people who follow, like and share relevant content. She'd found industry sites, social groups, real life groups, events, trade publications and online platforms that all had the potential to house their target market. He clocked a copy of the same document on Alex's desk. Dan started up his computer and sent Alex an email:

Alex, Sarah's left the overview doc on your desk. What are the chances I can have your thoughts on initial campaign ideas before close of play today?

Thanks

D.

He then worked his way through his emails, realising how

much stuff he was cc'd into that he really didn't need to be involved with. Having a stronger, dedicated management team would really alleviate the daily grind of running the business. As the team started filtering in and Dan was reaching the bottom of his emails, he saw Alex making his way over, giving him the thumbs up.

"Hey Dan, no problem for later today. I saw this last night, as Sarah emailed a copy as well, so I started thinking through some ideas. I'll share them with you before the end of day. They'll be in draft form though, that OK?"

"Yes, that's fine, I just need some ideas about the direction we'll take, for now."

"Cool, catch up later."

Next through the door was Sarah.

"Thanks for staying behind last night to get this sorted, Sarah. How did you come up with so many ideas?"

"Oh that's OK. It was just a case of putting myself in that person's shoes and thinking to myself, if I were this person where would you find me and how could you get a message in front of me? Once I had that clear in my mind, the rest was all research and ideas."

"Great work. Book in a few days extra holiday, if you like, to account for the extra hours you've been putting in."

"Thanks so much," Sarah smiled.

Later that day Dan an email from Alex arrive in his inbox, and he opened it eagerly.

Some early ideas. Let me know what you think - maybe we should chat through later today or tomorrow?'

A

Dan opened the attachment and started reading Alex's plan to build their employer brand.

Alex's plan to build an Employer Brand

- Develop a specific careers page as a subdomain on the website.

- Use pictures of the team in a 'meet the team' format as content on the page.

- Utilise a carousel function with 'Why I Work for Trolley Deals UK'. Interview a handful of team members to talk about why they work for the business. Maybe even a video, 'behind-the-scenes' style.

- Use the research on their competitors' employer brand and create a brief SWOT analysis. He highlighted what they were doing well, and where and how Trolley Deals UK could do better.

- Create a monthly blog focusing on a specific team member, or department in the business. The department chosen then correlates with the current hiring priorities.

- Target specific interest groups on social media platforms - even building their own 'careers' social media group.

- Social media careers pages to be informative and tell a story, not just be a jobs feed.

- Off-line events they could sponsor and conferences they could attend.

He had also composed paragraphs in a test 'voice' that would appeal to this specific demographic, and noted that there was

THE RECRUITMENT REVOLUTION

even an industry employment award they could apply for to help with raising their profile as an employer of choice.

Dan could feel his excitement brewing. How had he not thought of his recruitment like this before? He was so ingrained in seeing recruitment as a transaction instead of an interaction, it was no wonder they weren't getting anywhere. It wouldn't happen overnight; it would take timing, planning and precision, but this was a great start.

Dan emailed Alex back.

Love it. Let's get something in the diary to start planning the execution later this week. Please liaise with Sarah. Great work!

D.

5 Key Takeaways from Step 3

1. Define **who** you are looking for and really get into the details. Where will you find them? What do they like, dislike, eat, do with their free time and so on? Get clear on this picture to build your strategy.

2. **Where** will you find this person? Can you access them through social media, real life events, specific websites or industry publications?

3. **How** will you then target them? Build a strategy to engage with them based on **where** you think you'll find them. Is it through paid-for social media campaigns, a blog post in an industry publication, or sponsoring or appearing at an event or conference? Develop a voice and messaging that will engage them.

4. Get to know your competition. Research and understand how your competitors are positioning their jobs and decide what you could emulate and what you could do

better to build your unique employer brand.

5. Build your platforms. A careers page, social media strategy and applying for awards are just some of the ways you can build a 'green light always on' evergreen recruitment marketing campaign to consistently attract passive candidates.

CHAPTER 5

Dan was ready and waiting for Anna in the usual spot at the usual time with the usual drinks. As always, he was a minute or two early and Anna arrived precisely on the hour, waving as she approached the table.

"Dan. How's your week been?" She placed her bag on the floor and sunglasses on the table.

Dan smiled. "Hi Anna, good to see you again. Well, it's really coming together. We've got a huge amount of work done towards the recruitment marketing project, in terms of establishing and building our employer brand. I'm lucky to have a great team around me."

"Great, I'm pleased for you. I'd love to see some of what you've done."

Dan showed her the highlights of the research, Alex and Sarah's ideas and finally his own thoughts and feelings. "But we've still got some work to do in terms of refining and executing," he concluded, folding the paperwork back into the file.

"I think it looks good. If you're able to deliver in the way your plan sets out you'll have a compelling employer brand, and longer term you'll start to see a spike in interest from your organic recruitment. But just remember: it won't happen overnight"

Anna took a sip of her coffee.

"I feel we've got this element under control for now: Alex, Sarah and I will be working behind the scenes to get the wheels in motion, ready to launch in the next few weeks. What's the next thing I need to focus on?"

"Well, you will need to get your careers site up and live as part of your recruitment marketing. Remember that's your shop window; if you don't get that right, we won't see the results you're hoping for."

"OK, understood. I'll get Alex to prioritise that this week. To be honest I'd rather have the start of something live and ready to go, and then we can tweak as we test and measure in terms of what sees the most engagement. Exactly as we do with our marketing campaigns."

"Exactly. And when that piece of work is completed, the next area we'll look at is how to build an internal talent pool."

STEP 4. AN ENGAGED INTERNAL TALENT POOL AND NETWORK-BUILDING

"This is something we've always tried to create but we've never managed to establish a process that sticks."

"That's not unusual, because it requires consistency," Anna said, "but it's key in building a long-term talent attraction and engagement strategy. It isn't a short-term project: it could take years to build a pool of appropriate and engaged talent, but if you are in the business for the long term you will reap the rewards."

"So, what's the secret?"

Anna smiled. "As with all areas of recruitment, there is no secret. It's just about good systems, consistency in communication and engaging with talent. It leads back to your employer branding work. Picture this: a potential candidate finds their way to your careers page, loves everything you stand for and wants to come and work for you. They look through your current vacancies and opportunities but can't see anything that matches their skills and experience. As things stand now, what happens to those people in your business?"

Dan sat forward in his seat. "Actually, we do have a specific careers email address that we advise people to send a CV to."

"Well that's a start. What happens to those CVs next?"

"Sarah looks after the inbox. Occasionally she'll send a CV to me if it looks good or it's a role we're recruiting for, but other than that, I'm not sure."

"This is the first thing we need address. Where are those CVs going? Are they just sitting in that inbox?"

"Probably," Dan confessed.

"Well, they're useless there. The purpose of a talent pool is to maintain a diverse range of talent at any one time because, ultimately, talent pools must be future thinking. It's not about who you're hiring for today, but who you might be hiring for tomorrow. This is the start of their journey with you as a potential employer but the way you are currently managing this pool of potential future employees means it's potentially the end if you don't have a role for them today, or their CV doesn't catch your eye quickly enough to engage with them. Once you start to build it, you've got to engage with it."

"But how can we keep people engaged for longer than they are looking for a job? Presumably if they've opted into our talent pool, it's because they're looking for a job right now?"

"You're right, but you need to start to take a longer-term

view on your relationship with potential candidates. If they no longer want to hear from you, if you don't find them a role before someone else does, give them the *option* to opt out. But I bet you'll find that somewhere in the region of 80% will want to stay engaged with you."

She paused for a sip of her drink.

"The candidate mind-set has evolved: a 'job for life', or even a job for more than five years is a wholly out-dated idea. You need to be thinking about how you engage with candidates for the entire duration of their career. You might not have the right opportunity this time around, but perhaps by the time they are next looking the timings will align and you'll have an engaged candidate waiting in the wings; right place, right time."

"So you're saying that we should be building a pool of candidate CVs not of people that necessarily match the roles we're hiring for *today*, but with a view that anything could happen in the next five years, preparing ourselves for any and every type of talent we could possibly need?

"Exactly."

But how can we manage that? How does that become an asset rather than a burden?"

"Good question. It's all down to how you manage it. My suggestion would be that you automate the process using systems. We'll talk about systems further down the line, as it's one of the final things you'll want to consider, but depending on the volume of potential candidates you acquire, there are several manual systems you can use.

The first is a simple spreadsheet. Broadly speaking, any candidate who sends in a speculative CV and looks as though they *could* work for you at some point, or applies for a job but they aren't quite the right fit, goes in the spreadsheet.

- Choose simple categories that will easily sort the candidates.

- Input sort formulas for each column.

- When a new role becomes available, this is the first place you search.

She continued. "Then in terms of the CVs you need to make sure you are storing them in a secure file, in line with your privacy and data protection policies."

Dan leaned forward to look. "OK, that makes sense, but it does feel quite manual. Are there any smarter ways to manage it?"

"There are always plenty of ways to skin a cat," Anna smiled. "An alternative is using talent banking software, either as a standalone product or as part of a recruitment system: an Applicant Tracking System, or ATS for short. We'll talk about how an ATS can help and what it does another time, but for the purposes of this conversation you can buy or build talent banking software that allows candidates to upload themselves into the recruitment system, via a portal or application process on your website. Once they've done this you can search those candidates against keywords related to the job."

"That sounds a bit more like it. I can see how the spreadsheet method would work for some businesses, but we probably have the in-house capability to build a basic system along those lines."

"Hang fire until we talk ATS in a few weeks' time," Anna laughed.

"OK, OK I'm getting carried away. So, I'm now starting to build this pool of talent, potentially full of people I might not speak to for a couple of months or even a couple of years. What do I do next?"

"This is where many companies fall, when trying to build an effective and useful talent pool. They forget to *engage* with the talent, and the whole process becomes fruitless. There are several ways you can engage with talent, but my strategy would be focused on:

- Regular, value-add digital communications.

- A monthly e-newsletter or bulletin filled with interesting content around your business, your industry and your current open vacancies.

- Encouraging the pool to share content with friends and family to build a community.

- Starting a relevant hashtag, or encourage followers to share content on their social media.

- Making your talent pool feel like they are part of something."

"Exactly as we'd do for a business marketing campaign," Dan shrugged.

Anna nodded.

"Certainly something we can make a start on and look to improve with time," he agreed.

Anna paused for a moment, then added, "One other consideration in this Dan, is your *internal* talent marketplace."

"Sounds intriguing; how does that work?"

"It's a complex concept, but the idea that sits behind it is understanding the talent and resource you already have internally, and building on that to future-proof your business."

She took a sip of her drink and continued.

"It's about up-skilling members of your team in the areas of your business you deem to be mission critical, and thinking about your team as a more fluid pool of talent, instead of each person remaining in one blinkered lane, attached to one job title. Think of it like a cross-pollination strategy. In line with your wider business planning and business strategy, consider the roles that would be crucial in a crisis, time of upheaval, change, or simply an incredibly busy period, and consider how you could internally and sustainably up-skill certain members of your existing team, from other areas of the business, to be ready for that challenge. It's a way of future-proofing your business, but also developing your team."

Dan was nodding. "Sounds interesting. Where would we start?"

"Here's what I would do:

- Start by studying your business plans for the next few years, identifying the areas of potential growth and risk. Highlight where staff resource would be needed within the business on that basis.

- Look at the talents and capabilities you already have within your team. Do you know them well enough? Is anyone being underutilised?

- Start to look at members of the team that could potentially skill-swap. This won't work with every area of the business - you probably won't have a skilled engineer who could suddenly become a marketing guru - but look for areas of natural cross pollination in skills, whether based on the department they were hired to work in or an underutilised skill that could be developed.

- Once you've identified the areas in the business that may require more resource, based on the future business plans and the team members that could skill share, set up a part time secondment-style scheme.

- I suggest looking at team members swapping for a couple of hours or half a day per week, while undertaking their day job in parallel as opposed to a traditional secondment, which involves internal movement on a fixed term contract, full time into that new role. This can be great but it creates a constant problem with backfilling the role every time a person moves on.

This strategy starts to future-proof your business, and it's particularly useful if your path suddenly hits an unexpected bump and it's all hands to the pump. If you've identified the right potential issues and the right pairs of hands, you'll sail smoothly through any crisis and change - at least from a people perspective."

Dan was absorbing all this valuable information. "I love this. We do have a skilled team, and maybe there are some underutilised people there. The nature of what we do lends itself to this cross-pollination strategy. It's certainly one to think about."

He looked at his watch.

"Looks like time's up for today. Quick recap?"

Anna smiled. "Of course. Ahead of next week, here's what I'd like you to do."

Dan's Homework - Step 4

1. Work out what is happening with speculative applications at the moment, and get to grips with the current process for the speculative applicants (if there is one).

2. Start to plan how the talent pooling process will look, both from your side and that of the candidate. Start with how they can apply, then think about how you will keep them engaged.

3. Plan a communication strategy. Once we start to build this pool of talent, how will we engage with them? How regularly? What content will we use? How will we measure its success?

And bonus homework number 4: how can you build an internal talent marketplace to future-proof your business? Just start to think about it at this stage.

"Clear?" Anna asked.

"Yes. One thing, though, to clarify: this stage is just planning the talent pool and working out what happens to speculative applications, yes? We're not actually building it yet because it will become part of the bigger recruitment system?"

"That would be my recommendation, yes. It takes some time to get these things right, to ensure a great user experience and a streamlined and cohesive process."

"Understood. I'll start with the tasks you suggest and hopefully, by the time we get up to speed with systems and processes, we'll have a clear picture about what the talent pool looks like."

Anna stood up. "Excellent work, Dan. Have a great week and I'll see you next week?"

"See you then."

Dan walked back to the office in the late summer sunshine, thinking how far he had come in the process already, and how differently he felt about recruitment. He had never appreciated how much work it took to pull all the different elements together. Previously he'd scoffed at businesses with internal recruitment teams, thinking it was an indulgent luxury. But, now he'd started to look at the process and strategy in this much detail, it was easy to see how this could be a full-time job.

He arrived back at the offices as the team were nearing the end of their lunch break.

Sarah was at her desk with her headphones in, eating from her veggie salad box. As Dan headed back to his desk she pulled her earphones out. "How'd the catch up with Anna go?" she asked.

"Thought-provoking as always," he answered. "Are you on lunch, or have you got a second?"

Sarah put her headphones down. "Both."

Dan smiled. "OK good. What happens to job applications that have been made speculatively or for a specific job but they haven't been successful?"

Sarah put her fork down and fired up her screen. "Well, as you've seen, if anyone looks interesting, regardless of whether we're advertising for that particular role, I'll always send them straight to you. Obviously if we are hiring I'll send CVs with any potential to the person who's hiring for the role. From there, I guess it's up to them what happens with them."

"And we've got a 'careers@' email inbox where all of these CVs land?

"Exactly."

"Can you send me the log-in details for the account?"

"Done."

"Great, thanks."

All the log-in details were already in his inbox when Dan sat down to work again.

5,678 emails. Anna was right; this would be a sizeable job to get started with.

He started flicking back through the emails, noting that a few them were back-and-forth conversations between candidates and Sarah. The applications went right back to the very start of the business. There really was little point in engaging with prospective candidates from so far back, and after such a long period of time, he thought. This was an oversight he wouldn't make again.

WHAT DAN DID - STEP 4

Based on the volume of emails, Dan decided to look back over the last six months of them, and find the CVs. Any interesting ones with potential for current or future roles in the business, would go into a protected file, and the basic details put into a spreadsheet. The next task would be to find out what happened with each candidate: were they interviewed? Were they rejected? Did they receive any contact at all?

Once the status of the applicants was established, the team could get in touch to see whether they wanted to remain in contact with the business. Then the final step would be to develop a contact schedule and create engaging content for a monthly newsletter. Assuming that a wider recruitment system would be built in due course, a function could be built in to store these candidates within a searchable portal. They could then pull the data and put it into an automated email marketing programme to create and send out content.

"Sarah," Dan called over the desk. "Next phase of the

recruitment project - do you have 10 minutes now to chat through it?"

"Sure," Sarah said, gathering her notebook and making her way over to the meeting room with Dan. Once the door was closed, he explained the next steps to her.

"The idea is that although it won't necessarily plug the gaps for now, we'll start to build our own internal group of candidates, that we put into the pool because they might be right for future roles. We keep them engaged, interact with them and keep them up to date with all our current opportunities."

"That's brilliant. I'd always wondered what we could be doing with all the candidates just sitting dormant in the inbox. Plus, you never know who they know - we should be also encouraging them to share opportunities across their social networks and with friends and family."

"Good idea, yes. We can make it easy for them to share across social media and remind the pool to think about who they know, who might want to know about the role." Responded Dan.

"I'm on board. We'll just need to look at my workload," Sarah gave him a strained smile. "I'm busy with work supporting you, and now I've taken on the recruitment work as well. I enjoy it, but it's hard work. This is now another big project to undertake and I need to be realistic about timeframes and what I can achieve."

"Completely understand Sarah, and I appreciate your honesty. This is important, but not urgent. Anna suggested we just start to *think* about how this will work, but don't properly implement the process until we have our processes and systems in place, to ensure everything works in cohesion. But I hear you when you say you've got a lot on right now: let's monitor it, let's keep talking, and if you start to feel overwhelmed we'll work out a plan to make sure you're supported. I'll also have a chat with Anna, if you don't mind, to see what she would suggest."

"Thanks Dan, I really appreciate it. I'll schedule some time in later this week to start pulling CVs from the inbox from the last six months, and we'll go from there."

"Even next week's fine if you're swamped; just let me know how it's going and what I can do to help."

They left, and Dan headed for the doors to make a call to Anna. She answered after a couple of rings. "Dan, how's everything going?"

"Not too bad, we're looking at how we structure our talent pool and identify whether we've missed out on any potential candidates along the way. I made the decision to only go back through six months of applications: more than that just felt like we might be wasting our time?"

"Yep, agreed." Anna said.

"The issue we're having is with time. We are struggling to find the capacity internally to do everything we need to. Sarah is busy, and I'm not sure there's anyone else in the team internally that I trust to delegate this stuff to at this stage. I'm happy to lead the direction of the piece of work, but I don't have the bandwidth to execute it. How do you suggest we might manage it all?"

"This is a common problem, once we start to pull apart the logistics of running a successful recruitment function." Anna said. "What you might find is that longer term you'll need to build a Recruitment Co-ordinator or Recruitment Manager into your hiring plan - but that isn't what you need right now. Firstly, you need to make sure that Sarah's time is being spent in the right places. I understand that you don't want her to delegate the recruitment work, but does she have other work she can offload, or streamline to give her more available time?"

"Probably. I'll ask."

"Your second option is to outsource some of the work. If it would help, I'm finishing up on a couple of projects later this month, so if Sarah is still struggling to get the systems and processes in place, either I or one of my team can work with you a little more intensely if you need the extra support. Like an outsourced, in-house recruitment team"

"That could be an option," said Dan thoughtfully. "I didn't know you could outsource recruitment like that. I'd always just thought outsourcing recruitment was always through recruitment agencies."

Anna laughed, "I had assumed that in the time we've spent working together, you could see that there was a different way?"

Dan laughed too, now, a bit embarrassed to be picked up like this. "I know, I know - thanks Anna, that all helps. I don't want Sarah to become completely overwhelmed and leave, because of the extra work. We really need her."

"I understand. The best piece of advice I can give is to keep listening, and utilise automation, delegating and outsourcing to streamline her workload. Remind her that this is temporary. The bulk of the work is upfront - she could think of herself as a project manager to get this off the ground, with a view to bringing in a new team member to run the function in the future."

"Great way to look at it. See you next week!"

5 KEY TAKEAWAYS FROM STEP 4:

1. Talent pools can be as basic as a spreadsheet and secure folders, or as complex as bespoke software. Find what is right for your business and regularly review.

2. Take a view on the content of your pool approximately

every six months. Going back much further than that (unless candidates are pro-actively opting in) rarely yields results.

3. Look at ways to retain control of who sits in your talent pool and how they are categorised. Don't automatically link up a 'drop your CV off here' link on your website, for candidates to self-populate. You need to be proactive about filtering and filling the pool with talent that will be valuable to your business. A talent pool is only as useful as the information and content within it.

4. Don't let the content of your talent pool sit passively: engage with it. Develop value-added content, such as tips and blogs, alongside promoting your vacancies, to ensure that you are the first business your ideal candidates think of when the time is right.

5. How can you start to move away from rigid and fixed job descriptions for your existing team? While everyone has a place in the structure of the business, start to build a strategy for developing cross pollination of skills between departments and team members to future-proof your business and increase your internal capabilities, building an internal talent market place.

CHAPTER 6

Dan was looking through the first mock-ups of the careers page that Alex had sent over earlier that morning, when his phone rang. It was Neil, probably calling to check on recruitment again. Dan hesitated for a second and answered on the penultimate ring - not really in the mood for a conversation, but acutely aware of the responsibility he had to his enthusiastic investor.

"Neil, how's it going?" Dan asked, faux grin on his face to ensure he sounded upbeat.

"Absolutely fantastic Dan, just on our way over to Monaco after a weekend at the Grand Prix. Excellent weekend as always - Lewis is just something else. Very funny guy. How's things at Trolley Deals UK? How's the recruitment?"

Dan, dreading the question, responded, "We're getting back on track. I've bought in a consultant to help us through, and we've built a solid plan. I'm happy with the way it's shaping up for us."

"But what about actual results, Dan? How many people have you hired since we last spoke?"

Dan paused before he answered. "Well, none. But the point is, we've now got a plan. I've restructured internally, and started some of the dev guys on new training courses, which is already starting to plug some of the gaps from a more commercial perspective, so we aren't slowing on growth. We now need to think about our strategy to engage and hire future talent."

Neil was silent for a moment. "Dan, I think that is one of the most interesting things you've said about recruitment, since we've been working together. Completely tangible, great idea, totally on board with you. Who is this consultant? Sounds like they're a good find?"

"I'm not sure if you'll know her Neil, we met by chance in a coffee shop - Anna Rose?"

Neil scoffed. "Of course I know Anna - I'd have introduced you, but I didn't think you'd want to spend the money on putting a strategy in place. Great move, good investment."

Dan didn't let on that Anna's help was a favour. "Yep, it's been eye-opening and long overdue."

"OK, Dan. Well, just wanted to check in. All sounds good. Got to dash - speak soon."

Dan breathed a sigh of relief but was surprised Neil hadn't thought to introduce him to Anna, when he knew he was struggling with recruitment. He supposed that he had been blinkered when it came to hiring, not wanting to accept help - maybe Neil didn't want to be rebuffed and waste a good connection.

The following day was his next meeting with Anna, and for once she was there before him.

"Anna - great to see you."

"You too. How's your week been?"

Dan told her about their plans for a talent pool and how they would manage it, about some of the content they could use to engage with the talent pool, and some of his ideas for how they could manage the journey the candidates would go on - ideally automating as much as possible, but with a human touch.

"And we've already talked about Sarah," he finished.

"How's that going? Did you have the chance to speak to her?"

"Yes, we had an honest chat. We've got an apprentice who's been with us a couple of weeks, and although she's' still learning, she's bright and keen. Sarah thinks she can delegate some of her administrative tasks to her, leaving Sarah open to support me on other projects and project manage this. We've also got a strong admin team, and there's likely some resource she can pull on there too."

"That's great news. It can be overwhelming, but as we discussed, longer term you probably will need someone to manage all of this in-house."

"Noted. Does this put us in a position to start the process of hiring people? According to the forecast and strategy we put together, we need to start hiring by the end of this month to move things forward."

"Perfect timing. This week, we'll be looking at building your process, and over the coming weeks we'll go into the nitty gritty of what each stage of the process looks like. Once we've built the roadmap for the process, we can make a start in real time, with the live roles that you've got, while testing, measuring, and improving along the way. How does that sound?"

"Sounds perfect."

"Then let's start." Anna smiled.

Step 5 - Building and Documenting a Recruitment Process

"Tell me about your current process."

Dan put his coffee cup down. "It's straightforward, to be honest, and usually goes something like this:

1. Advertise role.

2. Post job on a job board, where we have a preferential rate.

3. CVs get sent to hiring manager.

4. Hiring Manager books interviews with the candidates they like the look of.

5. Hiring Manager undertakes said interviews.

6. Hiring Manager offers the job or carries on looking."

"Right. And how successful do you find this process?"

"I've never thought about it before. I always worked through a loose process in the way I'd seen it done before. We do get a lot of candidates who seem to drop out of the process pre- and post-interview, though." Dan said, thoughtfully.

"Have you ever thought about why that might be? Or asked them?"

"Now you're saying it, it seems obvious, but no. Sometimes candidates will volunteer that they've been offered something else, or they've been counter-offered in their current role, but that's usually unprompted and it doesn't consider other candidates who ghost us halfway through the process."

"Well, the truth is Dan, even with the most robust processes and systems in place you will still get candidates who drop off the radar during the process. If you get the process right, it should only really be happening in the early stage: pre contact or engagement. But there will still be the odd candidate that disappears into thin air after an interview."

She paused.

"What we *can* do is build in more candidate engagement and meaningful touch points to develop and build a relationship. Make them feel they are on a journey, and that interviewing with you is a great experience. This should result in deeper candidate engagement and a lower risk of disappearing candidates."

"Fewer candidates disappearing on us - I like the sound of that!" Dan smiled.

"Looking at your process I can see why you are losing candidates part way through: it's very one-sided. It doesn't present many opportunities to develop a relationship, and you aren't giving candidates the opportunity to get to know you. In their minds you are just another faceless high-growth, tech business in the merry-go-round of the job search they are currently on."

Dan thought for a moment. "I can see why you'd say that. We might feel that we're offering a good experience for prospective candidates, but we're busy and sometimes candidates get left out in the cold. It's often about what suits us, and on our terms. That's the way I've always thought of recruitment: that the candidate is interviewing for a job with us."

He paused to consider his trail of thought.

"My business will be paying them a wage to do a job in a good company that takes care of its people, and if they are interested in working for us they need to bend and mould to fit our needs from the get go, accepting that we are busy and might not be able to call them back quickly, or need to change interview dates at the last minute. Otherwise it isn't going to work long-term."

Anna visibly grimaced.

"Have I said something wrong?"

Anna took a breath. "It's not *wrong* to have pride in the people you want for your business. Nor is it wrong to be clear from the early stages about the attitude you are looking for from prospective candidates. But you must have a strategy to manage your assessment of that. Being honest with yourself, is your statement really an excuse? Because what you've just said doesn't assess a candidate's capacity to adapt to your business. Can I be blunt?"

Dan nodded, looking apprehensive.

"It sounds to me like an excuse for an inadequately managed and planned recruitment process, the result of which is disengaged candidates. You haven't assessed whether or not they could meet that criteria, because you didn't bring them far enough along in the process to have the opportunity to make that call."

Dan was silent for a few moments as he considered what Anna had just said.

"I think you've just hit the nail on the head, Anna. Unless we've proactively put something in place that tests and measures for flexibility, we are just leaving it to chance and not accepting that perfectly good candidates might become frustrated with us and drop out of the process, regardless of their natural aptitude to flexibility. So, what do we do about it?"

"We build a process that tests and measures for the attributes we are interested in, but keeps candidates engaged at the same time."

THE STAGES OF THE RECRUITMENT PROCESS

"Good recruitment - recruitment that reliably and continuously delivers - is a process. People don't like to hear that because processes aren't the most engaging subjects. But equally, very few small-to-medium-sized businesses get recruitment right. They're winging it each time and wondering why the results differ."

Dan agreed. "We do have a structure in place of sorts but it's loose, to say the least. Our other problem is who takes responsibility for what. I think that's often one of the biggest elements that lets us down."

"OK, let's work on that." Anna said. "Let's start with 'who takes responsibility for what.' How is that decided now?"

"Well, Sarah looks after the careers inbox - she is the first point of contact."

"Let me stop you there." Anna said. "Can I take you back one step further? Who decides what roles are needed and when? Remember we talked a few weeks back about recruitment forecasting and building a strategy? Who looks after that now?"

"Well, as you know we aren't quite that strategic about recruitment yet, but based on your guidance we are getting there. Until recently the managers have decided if the workload is becoming too much for them and their team and if they need another recruit. Then I'll look at the numbers, look at their request and make a decision."

"So, moving forward, who will own this initial piece of the process?"

"I will take the lead on recruitment forecasting, as I see it as a part of the overall business strategy, but I will still be guided by the team in terms of supply and demand. Ultimately, it will be my responsibility to oversee when who we hire, so we start the process before we're already on the back foot."

"Great, write that down. That's the first step of your process, along with confirmation of the ownership of this stage of the process. Then:

- If a member of the team comes to you with a hire that's outside your forecast, ask them to come back with a one-page proposal, so you know at a glance who they want to hire, why they want to hire them, what work they can do that isn't already being done and the cost implication, based on a proposed salary.

- Create a standardised template for this proposal, built into the first stage of your process. That way half the job of looking into the numbers and workload is done for you. Do sense-check the numbers, but this method gives your hiring managers accountability for proposing new hires."

Anna finished.

"That would work well. Anything to save me time and energy crunching numbers has got to be a good thing!"

"That is the first step of your process, which aligns with the work we did on forecasting and strategy. The next step of the process is how you define and decide exactly what it is that you are looking for. How do you currently do this?"

"When one of the managers asks if we can hire, they usually come armed with some kind of document outlining who they are looking for, qualifications etc and an overview of what the successful candidate would be doing in the role."

"Do you have a template they use?"

"No, they just come with the document. It's usually comprehensive as it's in their best interests to get the hire right. But no, there's nothing we've done to standardise it."

"Well, then that's Action Point Two, the second step in your process. This is your 'job description'. We'll talk about this in more detail when we start to break each element down, but in terms of the process, you need to create a standardised document detailing the responsibilities of the job itself, and the ideal candidate to fulfil that role." Anna gestured to Dan to make notes.

"That shouldn't be too difficult. Next step?"

"You tell me. After the hiring manager has come to you with their request for a new role, you've approved it - what happens next?"

"They write the advert. That's all on them: whatever they think is appropriate for the role. I ask them to send it to me before we post it online to sense-check. But apart from that, they get free reign."

"Well, the first step is to put an advert template in place, as with the job description. But some work also needs to be done in alignment with the employer brand guidelines we will create. Uniform format, agreed tone of voice and so on."

"That might take time and consultation with Alex in marketing, but I can see why it's a good idea, especially if we're developing an employer brand. All content will need to be totally on-brand," Dan responded thoughtfully.

"We'll go into it in more detail once we've got the process documented, but the advert is a crucial part of the process. I imagine it will take a little work to craft and approve," Anna said, nodding,

She continued. "We've got clarity on why we're hiring for the role, we've written the job description so we know who we are hiring for and we've got an advert, so we've really got the wheels in motion for attracting that person to the role. What would usually happen next?"

"Next steps for us would be to advertise the role."

"And where would you do that?"

"We use a couple of the generic online job posting sites, sometimes we put out a post on social media, and until recently we've still been using recruitment agencies for specific roles - so they take care of the advertising for us." Dan leaned forward in his seat. "But I know we aren't doing enough. It's evidenced in the results."

"I wouldn't go that far; you still do better than a lot of your competitors," Anna said, encouragingly. "Do you ever use industry-specific boards and networks?"

"Not really. Most of our specialist or senior roles tend to go to recruiters, so all of that is included in their fee."

"This is what I would refer to as the 'marketing, search and selection' element of the process. The key thing to remember is that every role is different, so every campaign has to carry a specific slant to achieve any traction."

"Hmmm. I'd never really thought of it like that before," Dan said.

"Think of it like this: if you're hiring for a Finance Manager and a Marketing Manager at the same time, you are talking to two different audiences. While I am making a sweeping generalisation, different types of personalities with different ambitions often work within relatively polar industries." Anna continued, "So while there will be exceptions to the rule, you need to consider your audience when you're building the campaign. Where will they find the advert, and what content will appeal to them?"

"I can see the sense in that. It is more work than we have put into this previously, but it definitely needs to be part of this process." Dan agreed.

"Right. So, let's say we've now started receiving applications. What happens to them?"

"They come in through the careers inbox and get forwarded to the hiring manager. Although, sometimes the hiring manager might put their email address on the advert so applications would go straight through to their email inbox."

Anna was nodding. "We need all of the applicants landing in the same place. As we've previously discussed, my suggestion is that we build an applicant tracking system, where the candidates can apply via your website, and end up in your recruitment system, which acts as the back end to your careers page. Here, you can move candidates automatically through the process. You can also ensure that all candidates who aren't successful receive a polite rejection email from you, which will help with your employer brand, and we can streamline processes for you internally."

Dan thought for a moment, "I'm sure we've got the capacity to build something like that in-house."

"Agreed, but remember it needs to be the last step in the process. We need to get the process set in stone so we're clear on the steps and the order of the actions before we build software to help us automate it. But it will remove the passing and storing of CVs in email inboxes from the process, which is a good thing."

Anna paused.

"Next question: how do you, or the hiring managers, know if the CVs are any good? How do you make that decision?"

"We just know. Gut feeling."

Anna looked at him, eyebrow raised. "*Gut feeling*? Gut feeling is an immediate response with no logical rationale; you get a gut feeling from a piece of paper?" she exclaimed.

Dan looked slightly embarrassed. "Well, we know what we're looking for."

"But what if someone surprises you? What if they haven't written a CV in a way that intuitively appeals to you? While I agree that you can make a certain amount of assumptions from a CV, for example deciding whether a candidate is *qualified* for the job or not, there's an awful lot of information you can't get from a CV."

Dan sighed. "But we don't have the time to scour every single detail on every CV that comes through the door. The candidates should make it easy for us to see whether they're the right fit. Surely if they don't and we overlook them, that's their tough luck."

"I agree that candidates should play their part in producing a great CV - but not all of them do. And, when you're in a shortage market such as yours, it's your problem if you miss out on a really great candidate." Anna said.

"I see your point, but how can we make this easier for ourselves?"

"Process. Putting in place metrics like a scoring matrix, a telephone interview or, at a higher level, we can even look at using psychometric profiling tools."

"A scoring matrix? How does that work?"

"It can be seen as a bit clinical or overly formulaic, and it needs to be done with a human element to be effective, but essentially you use the job description as a guide, and use the skills, experiences and qualifications to build a list of the ten crucial elements that a candidate will need to be successful within the role. Then, with each CV, you score them." Anna finished, jotting notes on a piece of paper as she spoke.

"Hmmm. Ok, and how that could work for us?" Dan asked.

"Really good question. Providing the exercise is undertaken with the right intentions, you are allowing your team to arm themselves with factual information as to why a candidate isn't suited to the role - based on the needs of that role - instead of someone just taking a look over a CV and making a more abstract decision. It means that if you were ever challenged by a candidate, you will have a paper trail and factual proof that the candidate wasn't right, and why they were screened out."

"OK, I see the logic. And what are the negatives?"

"The human element. Most people will probably have different opinions on scoring. You therefore have two choices: either one person does *all* the scoring, for consistency, or you have a handful of people - five or more - undertaking scoring, and the eventual score for each candidate is the average of all scorers."

She continued. "But there are lots of ways to uniform and streamline this element of the process. Let's have a think and we can discuss and agree the details over another meeting. I wanted to make you aware that the screening and selection element of the process can be done in many ways, and needs more attention than just a cursory look and a yes or no. You need to build in some consistency, structure, and some protection for you and your team."

"Agreed, we do need some consistency. I can see how 'gut feeling' might get us into trouble along the way. It's not tangible" Dan finished.

Anna nodded in agreement.

"So, where were we?" Anna paused. "Ah yes, the interview. Presumably by this point we have screened and selected our chosen candidates, and booked them in for an interview; what happens when they get into the offices?"

"I'm going to hold my hands up here because I know where you're going with this. There *is* no process, there are no standard questions, and if I'm not a part of the interview I don't know what has been asked." Dan said apologetically.

Anna laughed. "I feel like you're getting the hang of this. You've hit the nail on the head again: interviews do need to have consistency and structure to ensure you are running a fair process, particularly when you have multiple people interviewing for the same job. You need to ensure that every candidate is offered the same opportunity to showcase themselves within the interview. having a stock script that you can adapt for each different role will save your hiring managers hours in prep time, and allow you to standardise the process."

"As with all of the elements to this process, I can see that there will be some work upfront to get the templates and processes in place - but once we've got them it will make our lives a great deal easier." Dan admitted.

"You'll be surprised by the transformation once we've got everything in place," Anna smiled. "So after the interview, we move into offer and negotiation - tell me about that."

"It's usually managed by the hiring manager for the role, with some oversight from me. I sign off on the new hire, based on the feedback I'm given, and I sign off on the salary. From there, it's up to the hiring manager to make it happen."

"How does the conversation usually go?"

"It varies, to be honest, and some of it depends on the hiring manager in question - especially if the candidate wants to negotiate. This is often where I'm asked to step in, particularly for the more senior or specialist roles where we don't want to lose the candidate."

"It's an extremely sensitive conversation - in particular with in-demand candidates. They are likely to receive a number of offers and will use that to negotiate. A script will help, but also making sure you have the facts ahead of the conversation. I usually advise that the conversation about salary and any other perks that a candidate might be looking for is had in the early stages of the process. I recommend having that conversation during the telephone interview, so there are no surprises along the way."

"We have been caught out by that in the past," Dan remembered, wistfully. "It's happened to us on a few occasions, where we've found a great candidate and gone through the process, only to find out at the offer stage that they were looking for about £20K more per year than the very top end of our salary banding."

"That's exactly it - an open conversation in the early stages can save a lot of time and disappointment. It puts you firmly in the driving seat when it comes to this final stage. If you've each been open throughout the whole process and managed the candidates' expectations, the offer and negotiation stages simply become a confirmation."

"So that's it then - the whole process?" Dan asked.

"Nearly. The final stage in the process is often overlooked and can be crucial to the success of the hire. The Keeping In Touch schedule - or KIT schedule, as I call it. It's particularly important for candidates with a longer notice period, say for example, three months - but still important even if the notice period is a month."

Dan grimaced. "We've had candidates who've been counter offered by their current businesses or been offered something they perceive to be a better offer by one of our competitors. In fact, the first day we met, that phone conversation you overheard me having with one of our investors? That was about a candidate we'd been searching for, for months. The day before you and I met she'd accepted our offer of employment, and she was calling to tell me that her current employer had made an offer she couldn't refuse, and she would be staying where she was."

"Well, perhaps you've got something to thank her for? Our paths may not have crossed if that situation hadn't happened." Anna smiled.

"True. So, tell me about the KIT schedule?"

"It's straightforward. You plan specific action points to ensure you contact the candidate in the time leading up to their start date, all with the aim of ensuring that they turn up on day one, by building a relationship with them and keeping in touch." She paused. "And that, is the final stage of the process."

Anna went through the different steps of the process, in the order they had discussed. "By mapping the process out like this, we can see at a high level the steps in the process. Now we just need to go into each step in more detail and create the relevant documents and templates for each step."

Dan whistled. "Wow. We don't have anything like this. No wonder recruitment feels like such a never-ending cycle. Because we've never documented anything or decided a process, every time we run a new piece of recruitment, we start the whole thing from scratch. And that's probably why the results are so variable: we aren't clear on what we should all be doing; we can't put in place any metrics to measure the success and we're going round in circles."

The realisation hit him like a tonne of bricks. When it came to recruitment, they were busy fools.

Anna thought for a moment. "As I said at the start of this meeting, recruitment is a process. You can vary the specifics, you can trial, test and measure elements of the process based on what works and what doesn't. But if you don't have a solid process in place in the first place, whatever you try will never stick."

Dan's phone flashed and he was brought sharply back into the present moment, realising he was running late for his next meeting. "Anna, I'm sorry but I've run over into my next meeting. Is there any chance you can email me the homework?"

"Of course. Run. See you next time."

DAN'S HOMEWORK - STEP 5

Anna's email was waiting for him when he got to the office, along with a screen-shot of the process flow chart she had sketched in the coffee shop:

Hi Dan.

1. *Create your own version of the sketch attached. Does this process feel right for you? What changes would you make (if any?) and why?*

2. *Consider each step in the process. Who will manage each stage? Will the hiring managers continue to own*

this process, or will one person be responsible for co-ordinating it all?

3. *Document everything. As well as your own version of this chart, you'll need standardised templates and scripts for each stage of the process. We'll detail each stage of the process over the next few weeks, and we'll build these scripts as we move through that journey, but start to think about what will slot in where. and identify what you will need to build for each step.*

Great session earlier today. We've made real progress in moving this forward - I hope you can start to see the wood for the trees. For the next few session, we'll break each section of the process down into more detail. I anticipate these sessions will be shorter, so we'll start running the steps two at a time where possible - and I'd like to start running the processes in real time, starting with the roles you've identified you need to start hiring for.

Please bring the details with you next week of the new hires, and get ready to take things up a gear.

Talk next week.

A

Dan reread the message a few times. He was looking forward to putting everything he had learned into practise and moving forward with the recruitment, but at the same time he was apprehensive about how this would all work in practice. But he was putting his faith in Anna and her methods; it was time to build this process.

WHAT DAN DID - STEP 5

- Dan studied the process flow chart Anna had drafted for him. After some contemplation he decided to model his process on Anna's example for now and make changes, as necessary.

- The next task was to assign responsibility for each stage of the process.

- Dan decided that the hiring managers would continue to own much of the process. The key difference now was that they would follow a standardised structure. They wouldn't have to 'reinvent the wheel' every time they needed to make a new hire, and more importantly, the structure would allow them to continuously iterate the process, making improvements and adjustments where necessary.

- The final step was to identify where they would need to create a template or a script. Dan worked through each step logically and ended up with a rough draft of the flow chart and the appropriate action points.

Confident that he had made good progress, he hit save, closed up the office, and went home.

When he opened the door, he could smell already cooked food, and realised Emily had already eaten.

"Em, you here?" he called.

"Yep, just catching up on the latest episode of that show. There's food keeping warm in the oven for you - I wasn't sure when you'd be back." She said.

"I know, I'm sorry. I had a meeting with Anna this morning, and I wanted to get everything on paper while it was still fresh in my head," he said apologetically, as he entered their sitting room, where Emily was sitting. The remainders of her own dinner, clearly finished a few hours previously, lay on the coffee table in front of her.

"It's OK. I understand - this is an important time for you and the business - you've got to get it right. But it is getting a little lonely having dinner for one all the time. Maybe you can try and come home a little earlier once or twice a week?"

It wasn't an unreasonable request. He had been putting in a lot of late nights recently, and he could feel the strain on their relationship.

"Understood. Once this recruitment project is full steam ahead, I'll have more time to be at home with you. But right now, this project is all-consuming. It requires a lot of energy and resource - and it needs to come from me. As the Director of the business, it's my responsibility to build and shape it before the team can run with it. Can you bear with me for the next few weeks? I promise things will calm down and we can spend some time focusing on us. Take a holiday together, maybe?"

Emily shrugged. "Look, I've told you I understand. I'm just asking for you to try and come home to eat dinner with me a couple of times a week, instead of me spending my time alone. I don't think that's too much to ask."

"No, it's not too much to ask," Dan said, "but I'm trying to explain to you, that, for the next few weeks at least, I'm not sure it will be possible. This is a big project but it won't be around forever. Once I hand it over, I will get my life back. It will transform the business."

Emily sighed. "It's your choice Dan. It's always your choice. I'm on an early shift tomorrow, so I'm heading to bed. Enjoy your dinner. I'm sure we'll cross paths at some point over the next few days."

And with that she made her way to the bedroom, pointedly shutting both the sitting room and bedroom doors.

Dan sat on the sofa and put his head in his hands. He really hoped all of this would be worth it.

5 KEY TAKEAWAYS FROM STEP 5

1. A robust process is the key to building a successful recruitment strategy. If you don't have a process to test and measure against, you're reinventing the wheel each time.

2. Use a standardised structure and tailor it to the resources and people you have available.

3. Consistently test and measure your process, to enable you to keep the stuff that's working, and tweak what isn't.

4. It will take time and energy upfront to create the processes and structure, but think of it as an evergreen activity: once it's done, the first iteration is completed.

5. Don't lose sight of the fact that it's a live document: keep improving and tweaking to keep it relevant with the changes in your business.

CHAPTER 7

The first thing Dan did in the office the next morning was review his work from the night before. He was pleased to see that despite being so tired when he'd written it, he'd managed to create a process that was usable and ready to test with the first round of hires, even though it was only a rough version.

As per Anna's instructions he reviewed his priority hires from the recruitment forecast drafted a few weeks earlier and made a note of the hires that were needed urgently. Next, he forwarded his draft process structure to Sarah and asked for her comments, thought, or ideas. Just as he was finishing the email, Alex arrived and made a beeline for Dan's desk.

"Hi Dan, how's the recruitment work coming on? Are we ready to go live with any content yet?'

"Ah, Alex, glad I caught you. These are the first few hires we're looking at making. I'll have the full details of each role over the next few days, but can your team create content for our socials? Maybe some of those day-in-the-life pieces or blogs you suggested?"

He looked over the outlined priority hires. "No problem - send me the details when you've got them, and we can look at it from there.

"Cheers."

The office was filling up now and Sarah was also at her desk. She'd already responded to Dan's email to say that the draft process looked good and agreed that trialling and measuring was the best way forward.

In preparation for his next meeting with Anna, Dan started to write bullet points for each of the high-priority roles, over the next few days: the duties they'd be responsible for, experience they'd need to excel in the role and where they'd sit in the new company structure.

By the time his next meeting with Anna rolled around, he felt mildly smug about how prepared he was. Anna was prompt as always and grateful for the coffee Dan had already got for her.

"Thank you for the coffee, Dan. Now, tell me about your week."

"Honestly, it's flown by, but it's been good. I ran the process and structure past Sarah and she thinks it's worth trialling and measuring the success as you suggested. Let me grab my phone and I'll show you how it looks."

Dan pulled the attachment up on the screen and pushed it over to Anna. She studied the image, tracing the structure with her finger.

"Looks like a good first attempt Dan, let's see how it plays out. Now we've got a robust structure in place let's move on with the specifics and start populating each of the steps. Did you manage to dig out the recruitment forecast with the high-priority roles, so we can start to run this process in real time?"

Dan smiled. "I went one better: I've started to break these roles down and note what we need for each of them. The skill-set and experience a successful candidate would have."

He opened his notebook and started showing Anna his initial ideas and thoughts for each of the positions, and she nodded as he went.

"Great start Dan, well done. This is the perfect time to start talking about job descriptions and job adverts - not to be confused with one another. Let's start with job descriptions."

STEP 6 - A JOB DESCRIPTION DOES WHAT IT SAYS ON THE TIN

"I'll be honest," Dan said, looking a little sheepish, "I never knew they were two different things - I thought you simply wrote about a job and posted it online."

"It's a common mistake but there are some clear distinctions. The key point to remember when writing a job description is that it's like the skeleton or foundations of the role."

"What do you mean?"

"This isn't the place to do the big sell; that's the bit you save for the advert. The job description is an internal-facing document. It gives you the opportunity to be clear about the responsibilities and duties of the role in clinical detail. The very name 'job description' is exactly what it is: a description of the job."

"Ok, I'm getting the picture. Where do we start?

"By writing the reason why the role exists, in less than three sentences. No fluff, but a few sentences that summarise why the role is important to the business. Let's take one as an example and start to build a job description using that."

"How about the office administrator?" Dan suggested.

Anna looked at the notes. "Great. Why do you need an office administrator?"

Dan thought. "To free up some of Sarah's time on the administrative tasks, so she can work with me on bigger projects - like this one."

Anna smiled. "OK, maybe not quite so literal, but you're getting the idea. Let's take Sarah out of the equation. Imagine there was no Sarah."

He laughed. "Don't joke Anna - we can't function without Sarah."

Anna held her hands up. "OK, *hypothetically* no Sarah, don't panic. Anyway. Let's imagine this is a new role, why would it exist? What is its primary function?"

Dan dug deeper. "To keep the office running at optimum, and to ensure the team have everything they need to do their job."

Anna clapped. "Couldn't have said it better myself. That, right there, is your key responsibility and sits at the top of the page." She started sketching the structure of the document. Above the key responsibility, Anna also detailed the logistics of the role - its title, who the role reported into and the salary bracket.

Dan leaned over to get a closer view of her sketch. "So right at the top you put the core details of the role, followed by the reason for the role to exist. What next?"

Anna paused, sketching. "Next, we break down that key responsibility into 8 to 10 bullet points, which make up the wider responsibilities of the role. Give me one of the core responsibilities of the position?"

Dan looked at his list. "Making sure we have the correct office stationery and supplies when we need them."

"Great. So we detail that as: 'Ensuring that the office supplies, stationery and equipment are regularly monitored, replenished and replaced in a timely manner', or something to that effect. You can choose how you word it, but do you see where I'm going?"

"Yep, makes perfect sense."

Anna and Dan systematically worked through the list and turned them each into 8 bullet points to compliment the initial key responsibility.

"This is really starting to come together," Dan said, happily.

"It's a standard format, but most businesses just don't bother to use it - or they try and reinvent the wheel with the latest idea, thinking that a traditional job description is boring or out-dated. I understand the thinking, but the beauty of a great job description is its simplicity. A no-fluff document that clearly and concisely describes the role."

"I think this will work well for us once we get the template in place. So, is this the completed document?"

"Not quite. There is another element of this, which is the person specification. Again, self-explanatory: it simply describes the specification of the person you require. You can have them as two separate documents or roll them into one. The latter is usually my preference to avoid paperwork overload."

"The less paperwork the better, "Dan confirmed. "So how do we put a person specification together?"

Anna looked over his original notes. "We look at the skills, qualifications and attributes the successful candidate would need, or you would like them to have. We can break this into 'desirable' and 'essential', for clarity. But the one important thing you must be mindful of is ensuring that anything you outline as being 'essential' is related directly to the role, being particularly careful of attributes, as that can be subjective. We don't want to fall anywhere near the realms of discrimination." Anna warned.

"Absolutely not!" Dan agreed.

"Tell me one of the skills required from your list for this role."

Dan scanned his list. "Ah - excellent communication skills, written and verbal. Basically, they'll be answering the phones and dealing with various members of the team all day long, so they need to be confident with people and able to both understand and be understood."

"Great - so that would be:

· Excellent communication skills - both verbal and written.

Or something to that effect." Anna said.

Anna and Dan continued to work their way down his list, with Anna challenging Dan on some of the points he had written.

"How essential is it that they have a degree, for this role?"

Straight away Dan answered. "Oh, it's essential: pretty much everyone in the office has a degree. To my mind it shows a certain level of commitment, and to have a 2:1 or above shows a certain level of education and intelligence."

Anna raised his eyebrow at him. "I'm going to challenge you there Dan. For a start, I think that your opinion on degrees is old-fashioned. There are plenty of ways that people can get a great education through workplace learning, like apprenticeships and internships, and with the hike in tuition fees, university is more inaccessible than ever so some people can't access that level of education, simply from an economic perspective."

Dan listened.

"Secondly, it is not *essential* for this role that the person has a degree. What you need is someone who has administration experience in a busy office environment - ideally in a start-up or owner managed business. That will be much more valuable to you than simply someone who has a degree. Trust me."

Dan was silent for a minute as he considered her point. "While it makes sense, Anna, hiring graduates has always worked well for us in the past."

"Has it, though? Why are we here if it works so well?"

Dan couldn't argue with that. "You got me. Maybe you're right; it's something I've held onto from my corporate days and the fact that *I* worked so hard through university, where the pressure was always on to get into one of the top grad schemes. Perhaps I need to open up to the fact that the education world, and entry to the working world, are changing."

"That's exactly it. We can put the degree in the 'desirable' or 'nice to have' category, but make sure your own experiences, unconscious bias or limiting beliefs don't get in the way of finding brilliant people to help you build your business."

Dan digested what she was saying. She was completely right, and it was something of a revelation. The idea of thinking about what was essential for the job, rather than important to *him*, could open a wealth of possibility for candidates he may not have previously considered.

They moved onto the next two roles, flagged as immediate hires. They meticulously followed Anna's job description and person specification template to create three concise documents that detailed the description of the job to be performed and outlined the right person to do it.

She nodded.

"I guess that's it, then," Dan continued. "So where should we advertise?"

STEP 7 - WRITING A COMPELLING JOB ADVERT

Anna put her hands up. "Woah, not so fast. This is just the job description and the person specification. We've still got to write the advert."

Dan nodded. "Well, we've never separated the two out before - so this will be all new to me. Where do we start?"

"We've already finished the job description, so that's the first place to start. That forms the basis for the informational piece of our advert."

"Great."

Anna continued. "Next, we need to talk about the seven deadly sins of recruitment advertising."

Dan raised his eyebrow. "I'm intrigued - go on."

"The seven deadly sins of advertising a job are crucial in terms of engagement and ensuring that that translates to strong applications. These are the key things you need to bear in mind, before you write an advert for any job:"

1. **Confusing job descriptions and job adverts.** Two different documents, with two different audiences, content, tone and copy. Amalgamate the two at your peril.

2. **'We'-ing all over your content.** If your advert copy says 'we' more than 5 times, it's too much. A candidate isn't immediately interested in you or your business. They want to know what is in it for *them*. The copy of the advert needs to be candidate centric.

3. **Be clear on salary.** Don't waste your time or theirs. If you

know what you want (or can afford) to pay, then advertise it and make it clear.

4. **Be clear on expertise required.** As with deadly sin number 3, be clear on the level the position sits at and detail it accordingly. Allow people to self-screen themselves out of the process before they even apply.

5. **It's the perfect opportunity to sell the role.** Consider this advert your shop window as to what it will be like with your business - it's likely to be the first time a candidate has come across you, and your first chance to leave a lasting impression. Don't waste it.

6. **Focus on what you can offer, not what you can't.** Sure, you might not be able to compete with generous corporate salaries, but what *can* you offer? A 'bring your dog to work' day? An extra day's holiday for birthdays? An hour out of the office each week during work hours to attend an exercise class? Think outside the box for ideas that candidates will value but doesn't cost you anything except their time or a small concession to general practise.

7. **Don't ask too much of candidates.** Think of this as the start of a promising working relationship. Good candidates are vetting you, just as much as you're vetting them and asking them to undertake complex tasks or presentations before you've even engaged is a mistake. Save that for later in the process, once you've built trust and decided there is a mutual interest.

Dan was furiously making notes as Anna was talking. "Wow, that's a lot of information to remember for one small document."

"Remember Dan, this is probably the first time a prospective employee has engaged with your company. This is the taster - your chance to hook them in and intrigue them enough to read more. There is so much noise out in the jobs market, that if your advert is mediocre you won't ever get anywhere and you'll blend into the background - especially in your industry, where the competition is fierce."

Dan paused from making notes. "How do we put this all together?"

Anna smiled. "I like to break it down into six key sections:

1. An attention-grabbing headline - a statement that addresses the problem of your perfect candidate. Examples could be: variety of work, level of autonomy, security of the role. Whatever you think is important to your candidate, use that in your headline.

2. The introduction - briefly, what you're looking for and where the role is based.

3. What's in it for the candidate - why should the candidate apply for this job and for your company over any other?

4. What the day-to-day looks like - tasks, responsibilities, and expectations. What they'll be doing and why they'll enjoy it. This is where the job description comes in - but avoid a bullet pointed list of demands at all costs

5. The type of person you're looking for - skills, qualities, and attributes. The must-haves and the nice-to-haves. This is where the person specification comes in.

6. The benefits - Here's where you talk about salary, any benefits, and any nice extras you can offer.

Ideally keep to one side of A4, steer clear of waffle and make sure there are instructions at the bottom as to how the candidate should apply. If you want to, you can also add a downloadable PDF of the job description, which will give the candidate the facts of what you're looking for and the responsibilities of the role."

Dan cut in. "And what should we ask for at this stage, in terms of input from the candidate? Your seventh deadly sin was about not asking too much of the candidate in the initial advert."

"Good question! Depends on the level of the role. If it's a senior or specialist position, you might simply ask the them to give you a call or send an email registering their interest, making it as easy as possible for people to connect with you. If it's a technical or creative role, you might ask for links to a portfolio. But as a relatively generic rule of thumb, I would ask for a CV and a basic application form. You can even specify that it doesn't matter if the CV isn't up to date, just encourage good candidates to make themselves known to you."

"Interesting. What do you think about application forms, by the way? I always thought they were a bit old-fashioned?"

Anna thought for a moment. "Application forms are one of the most divisive topics in recruitment screening. Look, they have a place, especially in industries where candidates may not have CVs. Industries such as construction or manufacturing tend to benefit from application forms. The danger with an application form is that if it's lengthy, you might put good candidates off from applying. Particularly if you're asking for information like employment history and qualifications, when they could simply supply you with a CV. There really is nothing more frustrating."

Dan shrugged. "Makes sense."

Anna continued, "The positive of application forms, though, is that you can control the information you receive and you aren't given information you don't need to know about, or that have the potential to unconsciously sway your bias. Information like family situations or anything unrelated to the job itself isn't information you need to make your decision as to whether a candidate moves forward in the process - but if you give applicants free reign you open yourself up to being told information you don't want to know, nor need to know."

"Interesting. So, what questions would you ask on an application form?"

"I would ask questions that aren't obvious on a CV and will help you make the decision as to whether that person could be a fit for the role. For example:

1. Why the candidate feels they're a great match for the role.

2. A question related to the role itself, for example, 'tell us about x,y,z experience with x,y,z'.

3. A question related to work experience and/or attitude - for example, 'tell us about a time you went above and beyond for a customer.' If that's relevant to the role."

Anna paused for a sip of her drink, while Dan digested her suggestions and made notes.

He looked up. "We can definitely come up with something that works for us. I'm thinking, CV, succinct application form and for our technical roles - a link or attachment that shows their portfolio?"

"Sounds perfect"

Dan put his pen down as he completed his notes. "Before we finish, can we start putting together an advert for the admin role? I've then got some direction as to where we go with the rest of the adverts?"

Anna looked at her watch. "Yep, let's get at least a skeleton version completed together, and you could finish the rest and email it to me if you need to.."

They pored over the job description and person specification they had already created, populating sections three and four of the adverts.

"The key point to remember here, Dan, is not to just copy and paste bullet points from a job description. Remember we said the job description is the functional, internal-facing document? We now need to take that content and turn it into an interesting and engaging piece of copy."

"Noted."

Dan and Anna set about transforming the job description and person specification into a piece of copy that would really sell the role. It detailed what the position looked like on a day-to-day basis, made it clear that no two days were the same and billed it as suitable for a 'plate-spinner extraordinaire' who would relish the level of organisation and multi-tasking required to succeed in the role.

"Dan, do you have any notes from the employer branding work you're doing with Alex in your marketing team? We could do with manipulating some of the copy to create section two."

"I do indeed - in fact, I have the perfect paragraph." Dan smiled.

Finally, they completed the fifth and final section.

"Right, it's crunch time," Anna laughed. "What are we offering to entice people to come and work for you?"

"I've been thinking about this and I don't think there's anything wrong with all the ideas you've suggested. There's no reason why we can't offer a variety of things and start bringing it in with our current team. I love the idea of the 'hour out of the office for exercise' and the 'bring your dog to work' day. We could do it once a month. The team would love it."

"Day off on your birthday?" Anna suggested.

"That too! I'll speak to Sarah when we get back about how we communicate internally, because we'll need to let the team know before they see it popping up in an advert, but let's plan to do it."

They wrote the final paragraph about what a candidate could expect from coming to work at Trolley Deals UK, and Dan re-read it.

"Can we add something about working hard? I know it's not a big-sell item, but the reality is that we sometimes work long hours. If we've got a new update or there's an issue with the app, we don't leave the office until it's fixed. For some of our senior tech guys it's not unheard of that they've been in the office after midnight. Obviously, they can come in late the next day, or sometimes not at all and they'll just punch in a few hours from home, but that is the reality of our business and I don't want to gloss over it."

"No, you are absolutely right to bring that up; it's really important to give a realistic view as to what it's like to work at Trolley Deals UK. From what you've said, I'd say that's simply a grown-up working environment and you're in a high-growth, fast-paced business. You might ask for flexibility in working hours, but you'll offer it in return if it's asked for. You can elaborate at interview, but that's probably enough for a print advert."

"Perfect. It's important that candidates don't assume it's sunshine, rainbows and 'bring your dog to work' days - it can be a tough working environment and I need resilient people. People who aren't afraid of hard work when the chips are down."

When the advert was complete, they admired their handiwork.

Anna glanced at her watch. "I've got to dash, Dan, I'm running late - I'll have to email over your homework again, but this is a great start. Keep finessing and filling out the sections until you've got something you're really happy with, and email it to me if you want a second opinion. See you next week."

"Thanks Anna," he said, as she disappeared out of the coffee shop, knowing that the homework would likely hit his inbox before he reached the office.

Sure enough he saw the notification on his phone while he was walking back to the office. Anna didn't hang about.

DAN'S HOMEWORK - STEP 6 AND STEP 7

Great session today Dan. Ahead of next week:

1. *Refine the job descriptions and adverts we created today into two blank documents with guidance for completion for future roles.*

2. *Use the template to complete job descriptions and person specifications for all 'immediate needs' pieces of recruitment.*

3. *Use the template to complete job adverts for all 'immediate needs' pieces of recruitment.*

See you next week.

A.

Dan made a mental note to speak to Sarah about turning the new job descriptions and adverts into templates for future use.

As he made his way into the office, Alex was the first to seek him out, intercepting him before he made it to his desk.

"Dan, we're almost ready for go live on the new careers site. Can I send you over the links to the development pages for final approval? Also, did you have any job adverts we can post yet?"

"Awesome, can't wait to see it! Yes, I have the first advert ready to go - and I'll have to follow up with the next few. "

"Great, if you're able to send me over the advert you've got, we'll upload, and I'll follow up with the links for final approval."

"Nice one, Alex - really appreciate your help on this."

Alex gave him the thumbs up and headed back to his desk.

Next on the gauntlet run before he reached his desk was Sarah, headphones in, tapping away at emails.

Dan gave her a wave, and she removed her earphones with a smile.

What Dan did - Step 6 and Step 7

"How was your session with Anna this morning? I'll take it there's going to be work for me from it?"

"Intuitive as always, Sarah," he said with a grin. "Today we started creating adverts and job descriptions."

"What as two separate documents?"

"Yes, it was new concept to me too but it makes sense." Dan said. "If I send you my notes with the documents we created, could you turn them into templates with guidance notes that correspond - like an 'idiot's guide' of sorts?"

Sarah laughed. "Yep, forward it to me."

"Thank you. Once the templates are completed we have a couple of other roles that will need to be turned into job descriptions and job adverts. I suggest we forward each role to the hiring managers who will be responsible for line managing that role, along with the template and guidance notes. Then that line manager can complete the templates themselves. Kills two birds with one stone, as they will be given autonomy over the content of the role and we can test the templates to see just how user friendly they are."

5 KEY TAKEAWAYS FROM STEP 6 AND STEP 7

1. A job description is an internal-facing document and is intended to be a straight-talking, 'fluff'-free definition of the responsibilities and deliverables of the role.

2. A 'person specification' outlines the skills, experience and attributes of the desired candidate and can be a standalone document or part of the job description. It's also an internal-facing document.

3. The job advert is the external piece of copy, using the information gathered in the job description and person specification, written in a clear, engaging and candidate-centric format. Think of it as the shop window to your careers offering, written to attract a passive candidate. The candidate who isn't actively looking, but may be tempted if the offer is good enough.

4. Don't mix and match the two documents.

5. Don't simply copy and paste a job description (or any elements of it) and call it an advert.

CHAPTER 8

When Alex sent over the link for the new careers site, Dan found himself holding his breath with a certain degree of trepidation. He had such a clear vision in his head of how he wanted it to look.

To his huge relief it was clean, concise and slick, with images of his team at social events, professional-looking headshots of key members of the team popped up, and a revolving carousel of video, shot in their breakout room with the team talking about why they loved to work at Trolley Deals UK.

The copy was engaging, fun and friendly, but with a serious element to show that although they had fun, they also worked hard and needed people to join them on that journey.

Dan was delighted. He couldn't have pulled everything together better himself.

After congratulating Alex and the team, he gave a formal sign off for the careers page to go live. They had already put together a whole stream of automated social media posts ready to pump out job related content over the next month, to sit alongside more general business marketing.

Later that day, the site went live and Dan sent the link to Anna.

She got back to him within a few hours:

Absolutely fantastic - love it! Hope you're pleased?

Speak soon.

A

With Anna's seal of approval given, Dan spent the days until their meeting finalising the job description and advert templates with help from Sarah, and supporting the hiring managers to create their own job descriptions and adverts, ready for the next round of hiring.

They received an overwhelmingly positive response to the careers page from prospective candidates and their peers in the industry and Dan was exited to tell Anna.

She greeted him with a beaming smile. "Dan - I love it - you guys have done a fantastic job - how do you feel about the new careers page?"

"SO happy. It's the clearest I've ever been on our vision, and I have you to thank for that."

"You're very welcome. And how have you been getting on with tidying up the job descriptions and adverts? Any feedback from the team?"

"Actually, yes. It's been a collaborative process. Sarah and I delivered the templates and a mini training session to each of the hiring managers and asked them to create job descriptions and adverts for their specific roles, to take some ownership in the work."

"You're absolutely right to bring the team in at the early stages: not only are you able to delegate the work, but also bring them on the journey with you and get their buy-in from the start."

Dan sipped his coffee, looking more content than Anna had seen him throughout this process. "So what's next?"

"Well, everything we've developed so far, including the careers page, keep measuring, testing, tweaking and improving - based on the results and the feedback you get, both internally and externally. Now we've got our job descriptions and our adverts in place, we're going to talk about your marketing and search strategy."

STEP 8 - CREATING A CANDIDATE MARKETING AND SEARCH STRATEGY

"We're going to start by thinking back to a few weeks ago when you developed that ideal candidate. We take that persona and get even more granular, based on the type of role we're hiring for."

Dan was nodding. "OK - can we go through an example?"

"Of course. Let's talk about the new accounts assistant you need. We're want to attract someone who fits the target persona we've already identified, so, in an ideal world (and with time) your careers page and social posts will start to build an online audience that speaks to that target demographic - an audience of fans and followers, a community of people who like what you do, identify with your employer brand and would be interested in working for you, given the right opportunity."

"I see what you're saying, but isn't it leaving it to chance to hope that an accounts assistant will follow our pages and just be ready and waiting when the timing is right?"

Anna laughed. "Dan, you should know me better than that by now. Would I leave something to chance? We already know we need an accounts assistant within a 3-month timeframe, so we build content that will drive interest from that community. We share relevant industry articles, create a 'day in the life of the finance function' style blog, feature members of the accounts team on 'why I work at Trolley Deals UK', we focus on the areas within which we're hiring - or know we'll need to hire into - and build our recruitment marketing plan around that."

Dan digested what she was suggesting. "So, broadly, we need to start planning our content and strategy in line with the recruitment forecast we've built to start to organically drive the right types of candidates to our door."

"You've got it in one. That is the first arm of our marketing strategy. The subliminal and subtle piece. The next part is proactively advertising the role. Where do these get posted now?"

"Well, they go across the free platforms, and we have a digital job board we signed up with. Seemed like a good offer at the time, but I've never tracked back the return on investment."

Anna shrugged. "You certainly won't be the first or the last business to make that mistake, but we need to start getting more specific. First, we'll need to look at how that job board is performing for you. If you aren't seeing the ROI then reach out and ask why. I'm assuming they seemed confident when you first signed up that you'd see results, so let's make sure they're delivering."

"Agreed."

"Next," Anna continued, "We need to develop specific advertising campaigns for the specific roles. I'm not a huge fan of traditional job board advertising - I think it's expensive, difficult to predict and if it's not done with a strategy in mind it's the equivalent of throwing mud at a wall and hoping some of it sticks. If you are going to pay to advertise your jobs, you should consider either:

Using a specific industry source (website, publication, or news page for example) where you have the statistics to ensure your target demographic will be exposed to the advert, especially if it's passively.

Using a Pay Per Click (PPC)-style medium, where you can control the budget daily, track your results and adjust the campaign accordingly.

Dan nodded. "Makes sense. So how does the passive advertising piece work?"

"If you only advertise on a job board, you're assuming the person the advert is targeting will be actively looking for jobs. Let's face it, you don't go searching for jobs unless there's even a small part of you considering a move."

"True."

Anna continued. "We're ideally looking for people who are working for your competitors. Chances are, unless they're unhappy or we're lucky and we catch them at the right time, they aren't going to be spending their lunch breaks perusing job boards."

"I can see the logic in that. Aside from our own campaigns across the website and social platforms, how else can we get in front of them?"

"Well, this is where passive advertising comes in. Many industry news or even regulatory body websites will have an option to post an advert on a page not related to jobs, as a side bar to the top news story or a banner on the homepage. Some will even have a monthly newsletter where they add a well-crafted advert or advertorial in-line with relevant topics, so it blends seamlessly and doesn't even register with the reader that they are reading a job advert."

"But surely then that then misses the mark?"

"No, because it's about building awareness. The biggest issue you have in attracting the types of people you want is that they don't know you exist. Your ideal candidates are out there, plotting their next career move, and we need to get onto their radar - because you don't pick them, they pick you. It's about sticking our heads above the parapet to become an employer of choice, remember, and that doesn't involve shoving our advert copy onto the cheapest job board, crossing our fingers and hoping for the best."

"Brutal as always Anna, but I can't fault your logic."

"Of course you can't," she smiled. "So, what are we going to do about it"?

"Well", Dan said, sitting forward, "there are industry platforms where developers would usually hang out; I suppose the best thing to do is ask specific members of the team where *they* would look if they were searching for a new role. Not that I want to give them any ideas," he said only half-jokingly.

"Yep, good start. Anything else? What about the networks you already have?"

"Ok, yes, not something I've thought about much before. We occasionally get an email from someone we know already, who's in the right place for a move, or someone in the team knows someone who knows someone, but that's probably about as far as we've got."

"What about an internal employee referral scheme, which incentivises referrals with a bonus. It's easy to put parameters around it, for example only paying out once the new hire has passed a three-month probationary period."

Dan thought for a moment. "I've heard of other businesses running employee referral schemes fairly successfully, but I always thought my team didn't need an incentive to help the business. Shouldn't they be thinking that way already?"

"Maybe," Anna shrugged, "but most won't. It isn't because they don't care, it's because it's missing the primal instinct of 'what's in it for me?' But if you can incentivise it with a bonus, and communicate it effectively with your team, it will cost you a fraction of a recruitment agency fee, and probably less again than a paid job board advert. In addition, you will probably find that referrals are some of your most successful and loyal employees because they've been bought in by someone they trust, and a connection has already been built."

"That's true. Anything else can we try?"

"It probably wouldn't be as effective for this role, as this is an entry level administrative position, but for more senior or specialist hires we can also look at proactive search."

"Like headhunting?"

"Honestly, I think true headhunting is best left to the professionals. But we *can* search on job board databases and professional social networks. As a direct employer you will probably see a much stronger response than a third party agency, particularly through online platforms, so it might be worth investigating the potential ROI of a light level subscription package to allow you to search for and directly contact candidates."

"Noted. How about if we investigate the possibility of free trials on the professional social networks, or with a selection of the job boards?"

"Great idea - most of them probably will offer you that, and while you might not be quite as successful on the job boards with the more specialist or senior roles, you might see better traction and engagement on social. As we've talked about before, it's never one size fits all; we have to look at each role as a small individual project and work out which advertising and / or search avenue will deliver the best return on our investment - both time and money."

"Got it."

"Excellent. So, for this week's homework:

Dan's Homework Step 8

1. Create a documented employee referral scheme to motivate the current team to really dig deep in terms of who they already have within their networks that could be a fit for the business.

2. Build a plan for each role into a wider recruitment marketing and employer branding strategy for the business. Align all this activity with your recruitment forecast to start building a joined-up hiring and growth strategy.

3. Track your ROI on any current advert spend and make sure any money you are spending is working hard for you.

"Clear?" Anna finished.

"As always - absolutely," Dan said with a confident nod.

Anna started collecting up her laptop, paperwork and bags. "For next week, once you've refreshed yourself on your timeline of hires and you're clear on your recruitment priorities, start planning what each campaign needs in terms of a marketing and search strategy for each role. Feel free to boil it down to some high-level bullet points and email it to me if you need any support."

"Will do!"

"Have a great week and good luck with it." She waved and left.

Dan gave a low whistle. Time spent with Anna was always a whirlwind of information, and his brain was buzzing with ideas. He couldn't believe how far they had come in the last eight weeks - but he knew there was still a long way to go.

As he was making to leave, his phone rang. He didn't recognise the number,

"Dan speaking."

"Oh, hi Dan, it's, erm Julia. Julia Green here."

Dan desperately racked his brains.

"Sorry Julia, I get a lot of calls - could you just remind me how we know each other."

"Of course, sorry, we spoke a few months back about a Senior Developer position. At the time I was counter-offered by the company I was already working for and decided to stick with them."

"Julia! Of course, my apologies. It's great to hear from you - how can I help."

"Well the thing is, I haven't been able to stop thinking about Trolley Deals UK since we spoke, and now you seem to be everywhere, on my social media feed, side bars of the tech news pages - and I even saw the article on you in Technology Weekly. I can't get away from the nagging feeling that I've missed out on a real opportunity"

Dan smiled to himself. His team were good, and it was working. "Well it's excellent to hear our advertising campaigns are hitting the mark. I'd love to have another chat, yes. Things have changed quite a bit since we last spoke. We've reviewed our organisational structure and how we run our recruitment - so it might be a case of going back a few steps in the process to make sure we're a good fit for each other - would that be OK?"

"Of course, I completely understand."

"Excellent. I'll ask Sarah to make contact as to next steps and we'll see where things evolve from there."

"That's fantastic - thank you so much."

It was clear things were changing for the better and Dan strode back to the office with a spring in his step. He always felt much more positive and focused after a session with Anna, and to top it off they were already receiving contact from candidates who'd seen their marketing efforts - and it was still only early days.

Once in the office he made a beeline for Alex and the marketing team.

"Incredible job, guys, on the digital careers content. I've had a prospective candidate call me to say she might be interested in working with us. She would be a fantastic asset to the team, so thank you for all your hard work - it's already paying off."

Alex smiled. "We've been seeing lots of positive feedback too - now we've just got to get those roles up and live, so we don't lose the momentum."

"Absolutely. As far as I know we've had sign off and completion of most of the adverts for the first round of recruitment, so I'll have Sarah push everything over to you, and we can go live on the first batch of advertising by the end of this week at the latest."

"Perfect. Let's get this thing moving!"

Sarah was waiting for him when Dan got back to his desk.

"Good session again with Anna?"

"Yes, lots to think about. I've got a small list of actions for you in terms of research. Feel free to pull in someone from admin or operations to assist."

"Go ahead, I'm ready."

WHAT DAN DID - STEP 8

"OK, great. So, please could you:

1. Review the return on investment and any available statistics for the job boards and websites we pay for in relation to recruitment - number of applicants, quality of applicants, how much we're paying, that sort of thing - and put this into a spreadsheet for my review.

2. Investigate the cost of an online search facility such as a professional social networking site, or a job board relevant to our industry, as a tool we can utilise for all senior and specialist recruitment. Please establish where we can get free trials and set them up ready to use for this initial round of recruitment.

3. Look at the group of roles in this initial round of recruitment. Suggest and research where we can advertise each one, and whether the role is specialist or senior enough to warrant us proactively searching for and contacting candidates. I have some notes from my conversation with Anna on how to narrow this down,

4. Anna suggested creating an internal employee referral scheme. This is important, not urgent, but can you do

some research and propose how we could implement one?

5. Finally, can you send Alex all approved job adverts for the first batch of recruitment, and send an urgent reminder to the line manager about any outstanding ones. We need all the job adverts up and live by the end of the week at the latest"

Sarah was nodding and making notes. "This all should be fine. I can't see any reason why Lydia and I can't make progress on this rapidly."

"Thanks Sarah. Oh, one more thing; Julia Green called me this morning. The senior developer who turned us down a few months ago to stay with her current company? She wondered if she had made the wrong decision in the first place, and this was compounded by her seeing our new digital campaigns and PR work popping up all over the place."

Sarah raised her eyebrow. "It's a shame she wasn't confident enough to come to us in the first place. Amazing to hear how well the passive drip-drip effect of our new campaigns are working."

"Exactly. Could you give Julia a call to find out what she's looking for, what's changed and put the wheels in motion to run the new recruitment process with her? I've explained that she'll need to move through the process again and she seemed comfortable with that. Also, it'll be a good opportunity to road test everything we've put in place with a relatively warm prospect."

"Cool, I will take care of all of that. We'll have everything with you in the next few days."

"Are you ready to get those applications flooding in?"

"As ready as we'll ever be, "Sarah nodded.

5 Key Takeaways from Step 8:

1. Always begin a new marketing and search campaign by making sure your company's overarching target candidate persona are relevant to the role.

2. Consider what's appropriate for the level and department of the role: is it a more junior role that would be suited to a job board search and clever advertising campaign? Is it a senior or specialist role that will require a proactive online search and contact method?

3. What's your budget? Do you *need* a budget? If you are spending money on advertising, always do your research. Contact the advertising platform directly and ask them for statistics on your target demographic, for example, how many candidates they have registered in X industry or in X location.

4. Have you considered pay-per-click (PPC) advertising for your recruitment? It can be a good way of controlling your costs, quickly measuring your return on investment, and specifically targeting the right demographic of candidates.

5. If you don't have one in place already, an internal employee referral scheme can be a great way to encourage your current team to think about people in their networks who could be a great fit for your business. You'd be surprised how far a small monetary reward can go in terms of jogging people's memories.

CHAPTER 9

With confirmation that the wheels would well and truly be in motion on the first batch of recruitment by the end of the week, Dan was genuinely excited. Finally, recruitment felt fun again. Back in the early days of the business, when he still felt like he was just playing at being a Director, hiring people had been new, interesting, and like a game. But years of frustration, time wasting and rejection had worn him down. If he was being honest with himself, seeing all the work that went into running a proactive and strategic recruitment department within a business of his size, he had become sloppy and complacent, and it was clear to him now why he wasn't seeing the results the business so desperately needed.

Once they had mapped out and tested their processes, they would need to hire someone to run the recruitment for them. This was a job in itself and Dan couldn't afford to give up Sarah as his PA to take care of it forever. But he would cross that bridge when he came to it.

As he was running through his inbox, he remembered Sarah had forwarded him an email confirming the details of his travel and itinerary for the recruitment conference in New York.

Over the course of the next week, the first round of recruitment went live on the careers website and the social media pages of

Trolley Deals UK, and the response was astounding. Ordinarily they would expect to see an average of 1.5 applications for the technical and senior roles and 6 applications for office and administrative roles. By starting to build an audience, engaging with them and targeting them in a specific way, in a very similar way to how they would home in on, and target the prospective customers of the business, they saw an average increase of 250%. In some cases, and for some roles this was even higher.

But it wasn't just about the quantity. The marketing team understood they could cast the net wider and double that number again. What drove the success of their campaigns was the laser focus and clear understanding of the demographic of candidate they were targeting for each role. It meant that they weren't wasting time on hundreds of unsuitable candidates. Each application was tailored to Trolley Deals UK, carefully crafted by the applicant, and the buzz at how well it was going was palpable. Tired line managers who were working overtime just to complete the basics were enthusing over CVs of candidates they couldn't even dream had existed, and Dan knew that despite the time, hard work and effort that this project had been worth it. But the next challenge was what on earth to do with all these incredible people that suddenly wanted a job at his company?

Anna had been called overseas on an urgent client matter, so the weekly meeting had to take place virtually. As her now familiar face filled the screen, Dan could barely contain all the information he had to share with her.

"Dan - how's it all going?"

"We've had the craziest week. The first round of recruitment adverts has gone live and I have never seen anything like it," Dan was shaking his head in disbelief.

THE RECRUITMENT REVOLUTION

Anna laughed, gently. "All good I hope?"

"Oh absolutely. We followed all your advice and it's worked like a charm. Not just the quantity of candidates but the quality is now outstanding. We're at the point where we don't know what to do with them all."

Anna smiled. "Well, perfect timing - that was exactly what I had in mind to discuss."

Step 9 - The Candidate Shortlisting Process

She continued. "We're over the first hurdle and we've got some great people in through the door, which, if I remember correctly, is further than we've managed to get in a while?"

Dan nodded.

"Good. Now we're able to compare apples with apples, at last. But we want to make sure we stay away from our old friend gut feeling." She raised her eyebrow at him.

"Of course," Dan agreed.

"So, what we need to build is our selection process. Broadly, how do we move these applications from paper to people? We can't interview all of them, so we need to create our tools to differentiate between candidates to move them onto the next stage."

She paused to share her screen with him.

"Do you remember when we drafted our process, the first thing I suggested was this basic scoring card?"

The CV scorecard from one of their earlier meetings opened on the screen.

"Ah yes. I did like the idea. The main thing that concerns me is overcomplicating the process because we're all so busy, and if there's too much paperwork, it won't get done and we'll slowly but surely slip back into our old ways and habits." Dan said, uncertain of her reaction.

Anna nodded. "Completely valid point, and you are right. As I've said before, if you don't have the buy-in of the team, or your line managers believe that any part of this process is a waste of time, it won't happen. You don't want to have to supervise each piece of recruitment; you need confidence that it will be done consistently and to the agreed structure each time."

"Exactly. So, what can we do about it?"

"Well, my suggestion would be that at this initial screening point we create a set of standardised scoring cards. Either based on the department the role sits within, or the seniority of the role. The scoring card must be a mix of technical and competency-based statements and evidence of culture fit, recognising that culture fit is more difficult to score from a CV alone."

Dan considered this. "That is more realistic than expecting the hiring manager to create a new scoring card for every role. If we create a group of standardised scoring cards, attached to each department in the business, it means all the hiring manager needs to do is fill it out for each candidate when they initially look at their CV. In theory, that shouldn't be any more time consuming that simply looking at the CV and making notes?"

"Exactly. And so, this is also where we will need to create our application form."

Dan looked unsure. "I do agree with you on the application form, but how can we make still make sure it's a great experience for our prospective customers? We know from our own market research that from a customer perspective, the fewer screens and clicks a customer has to go through and the easier we make the buying process, the more likely they are to buy. It would make sense that the same is true of a candidate applying for a job?"

"I have no reason to doubt that you can make it cohesive, simple and relevant to the process. Internally, it will help you to screen more effectively and efficiently without ruining your candidate experience and hurting the volume of your applications. What it also allows us to do is add questions that are relevant to the culture of the business and the types of candidates you are looking for. We can then screen for the culture side of things much more effectively and truthfully."

"Let me have a think about that one," Dan said. "I'll speak to Sarah and see what she can come up with as a template. I can see how this will all come together, there's just a lot of moving parts at the moment."

"But equally, you could also make this work through plug-ins, apps and codes on your website, and some good excel spreadsheets. It generally depends on volume: if your recruitment is relatively low volume, both in roles and in applicants, you can get away with a more manual approach. If you've got several live roles and they are all seeing high levels of activity, an online recruitment system will ensure the process runs much more seamlessly. But let's test-run everything before we commit to building and implementing a system. It's much easier to tweak if we get it wrong the first time."

"Definitely," Dan agreed remembering his own painful, expensive and time-consuming software mistakes during the early days of Trolley Deals UK.

"In addition," Anna continued, "as we've mentioned before, from a compliancy perspective it means candidates don't give away any information that could spike an unconscious bias or lead to any claims of discrimination, because they are only telling you about the things relevant to the role as asked by you."

"Unconscious bias isn't something we'd considered before."

Anna laughed. "Oh it's rife, and because it's unconscious you aren't even aware it's happening. It can stem anywhere from feeling connected to a candidate who has the same name as you, all the way through to someone you perceive as being from a similar social group or with the same likes and dislikes. Especially with senior management, we sometimes refer to it as 'hiring in your own image': because you recognise similar traits and preferences to yours. Goes back to your old friend gut feeling."

"I'm sure we've inadvertently been guilty of that in the past. It's finding the line between culture fit and not hiring a group of clones."

Anna was smiling. "Culture not cult."

Dan laughed, "Exactly."

"Right. Let's trial an application form for all future applicants, and for the applicants we already have we will create a scoring card for each department, which can also be used moving forward. From a resource perspective, I suggest Sarah creates the draft application form and asks for each of your line managers in each department to create their own scoring card. That way, not only are you delegating work between the team for speed, but the line managers will ask questions relevant to them and have buy in on the process."

"Yes, we need to get moving on this; applications are coming in much faster than we anticipated. We've waited so long for a break like this, we don't want to lose momentum."

"Exactly - we're in a live process, let's keep momentum and energy high. Keep your team engaged and be clear with them that this work is urgent if they want to start growing their teams."

"Noted, we'll get that done. What else can we do at this stage to help us make the right decision and create the right early relationships with these candidates?"

"Once we've completed the initial screen based on the application form, I recommend we invite the first shortlist to a telephone screening interview:

- Approximately a 15-minute telephone conversation.

- The interviewer asks the interviewee a short script of questions to get to know them beyond their CV.

- This is the perfect opportunity to sense check availability - for example, full time or part time hours, salary expectations, notice period, and their understanding of what the role entails.

- The purpose is to screen for anything that has the potential to be a showstopper at a face-to-face interview, that can't be gleaned from their CV or application form, and to start to build the relationship with the candidate in the early stages of the process."

Dan was busily making notes. "And you suggest the same script for every interview, regardless of department or level of seniority?"

"Yes, exactly. You can leave some questions open-ended and skip past questions if irrelevant. The purpose of the telephone interview isn't to gather so much information you don't then need to interview them, but to help you make an informed decision as to whether the candidate has the potential to be a fit for the company and a fit for the role. There's no need to get too granular at this stage. Let me give you some examples:

- What interests you about our company?

- Why did you apply for the position?

- What are your current/most recent responsibilities in (x) role?

- Do you have experience in (x) software/programme/system?

- Would you consider yourself beginner, intermediate or expert?

- I can see a gap in your CV at (x) date - could you please give me some background on why that is?

- What challenges are you looking for in a new position?

- Why are you looking to leave your current role / why did you leave your last role?

- Are you happy that this is a full time/part time role?

- What are your salary expectations?

- What is your notice period / when would you be available to start?

- What is your availability to meet with us for interview?

Anna continued. "By asking these broader questions you get more insight than you could from a CV, confirm their interest in the role and suitability for the position, and begin building a relationship, which will result in better retention rates throughout the recruitment process and beyond into their employment."

Dan was listening intently. "Who does the telephone interviews, and where are they documented?"

Anna let a brief smile cross her face before responding. "Well, ordinarily it would be the central team in charge of recruitment, your recruitment or HR team. But as we haven't got that far, for the time being I suggest Sarah or someone from her project team could run them, or if you trust your line managers they can each take care of their own telephone interviews." She paused. "But I would suggest some oversight yourself on the notes from these interviews to check for quality assurance in the early stages of deploying the new process. In terms of where they are kept, I suggest for now that there is a master copy of the script template in a word document, which is edited on each call and saved against the candidates' name and the role they've applied for in a password protected recruitment folder. Longer term we can build this into your recruitment system, but as with everything I suggest we road-test the process and the script before we commit to building it."

"Sounds sensible." He thought for a moment. "I'd like to trial the line managers managing their own telephone interviews - at least initially. It will help to give them an insight into the information they can glean from the conversations, so when we do hire someone into the in-house recruiter role, they'll understand that the telephone interview isn't a substitute for a real interview, and won't be expecting a full scale debrief of the suitability of the candidate."

"That would work," Anna agreed. "I've often seen a recruitment process not moving forward because the person in charge of hiring doesn't make decisions quickly enough, because they don't feel there is enough information to make that decision. My general rule of thumb is that if after you've

- Seen their CV

- Seen their application form

- Spoken with them on the phone

- On paper that person could do the job,

- They're clearly interested in the role

- There aren't any glaringly obvious reasons why they wouldn't work within the culture or structure of the organisation

Then it's worthwhile moving the process onto a first stage face to face interview."

"Noted. And in all honesty, that's where we have floundered in the past: indecision. We've been quicker over the last few years, recognising that a lack of speed played a part in our recruitment issues. Anything else we need to be thinking about?"

"Yes, I would consider whether psychometric profiling is relevant for you. I've seen some companies use it as a successful part of their recruitment strategy and others failing miserably."

Dan thought. "It's something I'm aware of, but I wouldn't have a clue how to use it to make decisions in a recruitment process."

"It's tricky. People get hung up on types, letters and colours but have no idea how that is used to create a cohesive and diverse team. The worst are when business leaders decide they are using the testing to seek out a certain type of person or colour of person, and rely heavily on profile testing to unearth them, " Anna finished, taking a sip of her drink.

Dan shrugged. "Well surely you wouldn't want to build a team of clones - diversity, different traits and different ways of thinking are what makes a successful team?"

"Absolutely. If we were to add psychometric profiling as part of the process with Trolley Deals UK, we would first need to decide why we were doing it, and secondly for which roles: all of them or only Management, for example."

"Hmmm. I suppose my question is whether we need to utilise profiling at this stage, or if that's more of a team building future exercise?"

"There absolutely are arguments for both. There are some slightly more sophisticated candidate assessment tools on the marketplace, that focus on traits such as judgement and values as an example, but I think the human touch is the most appropriate. It's always something we can consider further down the line if it feels appropriate."

"Fine - let's park that for now. We've got plenty of ideas to move this stage of the process forward. I think we should start to move the candidates through, ready to meet us for a face-to-face interview. Not to pre-empt but am I to assume that will be the next step in the process?"

"Yes, that will be the topic for next week. If you can get your thinking cap on about what you want the interview process to consist of, that will be a good place to start. I suggest that once you've shortlisted your candidates you get them booked into interview slots for a couple of days after our next meeting, to keep that momentum going. I'm confident we can build an interview process rapidly."

"Anna this is just relentless!" Dan laughed, only half joking. "We can do it, of course."

Anna smiled. "Think about it like this: once it is done, it's done. We can iterate the process, tweak, improve and build systems later, but creating the process itself is the bulk of the work completed. I did warn you in the beginning that your timeframes were ambitious, remember?"

Dan chuckled. "I know, I know - never one to shy away from a challenge." He paused. "Before I forget, I'm booked on for the

New York conference."

"Fantastic. I think you'll enjoy it and meet some great people. You might even learn a thing or two," she smiled. "Right, time for me to disappear, but I think you have more than enough to sort out ahead of next week. To recap on what we've agreed today:

Dan's Homework - Step 9

- Create a standardised application form, and a scoring card that sits behind it.

- Create a standardised telephone interview script, which can be tailored by the user to suit the responses required for the role.

- Begin to think about the interview process. We'll go over this in more detail next week but look at what you have done in the past: what worked, what didn't and what do you think needs to change? Ask what you don't get from your current interview process that debilitates the decision-making stage.

And finally, you can start to look at potential dates and times for interview for the candidates you shortlist and begin to book them into the slots. Let's keep this process in motion!"

Anna began to reach for the 'end call' button. "Dan, that's us done - have a great week and I'll see you in the normal place next week?"

"Definitely. See you then."

As Dan closed his computer for the day, he reflected on how much they had achieved. Due to their tight timeframes, Sarah had pulled in both Tom, a junior apprentice, and Lydia to co-ordinate each of the hiring managers, andcreate standardised scoring cards and telephone interview scripts for each department within the business. They'd then co-ordinated diaries for efficiency and managed to book in all but a couple of the telephone interviews for the shortlisted candidates with the appropriate hiring managers, with a view to completion by early next week and face-to-face interviews in the latter part of the week.

It was already after 8pm when Sarah approached his desk. "What a day!"

"Tell me about it, but you guys have made incredible progress"

Sarah smiled. "Yep, we're pretty much there - it's a bit rough and ready, but it'll work for a first run and we'll learn lots along the way."

"Exactly how I like to work. Fail fast, fail early and make improvements along the way. If you get too fixated on perfection you never end up moving anywhere. How much have you all got left to do before you're happy to call it a day? Can't have you staying later than me," he joked.

"That's what I came over to tell you - all that's left to do is to book in the last of the telephone interviews. We're waiting for candidates to come back to us on that, we've left messages and we've got the slots available in the respective hiring manager's diaries. Lydia has just sent you the draft application form, you've already approved the score card and telephone interview script, so I think we are, dare I say, almost there." She crossed her fingers.

"Just one more thing - sorry!" Dan looked at her apologetically.

"Go on . . . "

"The next stage is obviously the interview itself. Because we've moved so fast we're running a live process in parallel with the build. That means that we'll be inviting candidates for interview, without having an interview process built. Likely another quick turnaround to pull it all together in time."

"OK - so what do you need me to do?" Sarah asked, folding her arms.

"Can you start digging out the materials we usually use, ask around some of the team what works, what didn't, what they want more or less of? Start to build a picture of what we need to be finding out from candidates at interview stage that would be useful to us moving them forward in the process, and remove that post interview doubt that we all usually end up with. Anna is going to coach me through the interview part with me next week, but has advised we get a head start on defining what we want, so we can build it quickly and keep the process moving."

"Makes sense. Yes - but it will have to be tomorrow now, I'm shattered," Sarah stifled a yawn. "I'm assuming I can keep Lydia and Tom with me as manpower to keep up? How did we end up running this so tightly in the first place in terms of timeframes and workload, anyway?"

Dan looked sheepish. "Do you remember back at the beginning when we built our recruitment forecast and I was convinced we could run recruitment at these volumes and build the processes and systems all at the same time? You and Anna did warn me it was ambitious, and it turns out there was an element of truth in that." He paused. "But we're keeping momentum: being live in process means there's pressure to get it done, which isn't always a bad thing."

"Hmm, "Sarah raised her eyebrow at him. "On that note - I'll see you tomorrow!"

"Thanks very much- excellent work today - see you tomorrow."

Dan was the only person left in the office now. In the silence he reflected on the day. He'd been impressed by how his team had stepped up to the plate and put in the work to make this happen. He couldn't do it without them - especially Sarah. She had shown herself to be extraordinarily resourceful, bright, capable, and supportive. He'd known before this that she was brilliant, but perhaps there should be something more for her at Trolley Deals UK than being his assistant?

Thinking he'd better make tracks to enjoy the rest of his evening with Emily he locked up the offices, set the alarm and headed for home.

This evening aside, he'd generally been getting home at something resembling a normal time recently - and it was paying dividends in his relationship. He'd sent her a message earlier that evening to let her know he was going to be so late, and as it was now such a rare occurrence she was much more understanding, and smiled when she saw him come in through the hallway.

"Good day?" She looked at the clock. "Thanks for letting me know you'd be a bit later today -it means I'm not worrying about you."

"Yes, this recruitment project is really picking up steam, and where I decided to implement some ambitious timeframes and deadlines, we're all hands on deck to keep up.' He called through from the kitchen as he took his food from the oven, "Thanks for this." He came into the front room and sat with her.

"I meant to say - I'm going to a recruitment conference in New York in a few months' time. Would you like to come? We could fly first class, stay in a nice hotel - make a mini holiday out of it. We could stay on a few days afterwards and have some time just the two of us? The conference is only for two days - so while I'm there you could go sightseeing, shopping - go to a spa, whatever you fancy?"

Emily beamed. "I would absolutely love to, thank you! I've got holiday to take from work so just let me know the dates and I'll get it booked in."

Dan smiled. "Excellent. Sarah is sorting it all, so I'll let her know our new plan and get her to send you the info. Anna is speaking at the conference and I know you'd love you to see her again."

"She has certainly changed our lives for the better, you seem so much more relaxed since working with her - perhaps we could all go for a drink or dinner one evening?"

"Sounds like a plan,' He wrapped his arm around her, as they settled into a cosy night. It was just the tonic after such a hectic day and Dan couldn't remember the last time all the parts of his world felt so much in synch and working well.

What Dan did - Step 9

The next morning Dan emailed Sarah about the changes to the New York plans before he forgot, and checked the application form draft Lydia had sent him. Only minor changes were needed, for it to go live. He forwarded this back to Lydia and Sarah, cc'ing in Alex, suggesting that once his amends had been added it could be embedded into the careers website as part of the application process. They were very nearly there.

Over the next few days the final telephone interviews were booked in. Only two candidates never phoned back, but Anna reassured him that that was par for the course, and nothing to be concerned about at this stage.

Utilising all the screening tools, job descriptions and a healthy dose of general understanding and clarity on what they needed for each position, the slots for face-to-face interviews started to fill up. Each hiring manager booked the candidate in to the interview slot via email and sent them an online calendar invitation with the date, time, location and other more specific details of each meeting: who the interview was with, the proposed duration and anything the candidate needed to bring or prepare.

5 KEY TAKEAWAYS FROM STEP 9

1. Decide what tools work best for you and the business to move the candidates from simply being names and words on a piece of paper to people in front of you in an interview. Consider a well thought-out, succinct and engaging application form and scoring cards to support your decision-making process.

2. Score cards are a great way to justify the decisions you make - they can easily be created in alignment with job descriptions and company culture statements, tweaked for the varying levels of experience and skillset within each team.

3. Always utilise a telephone interview as part of your screening process. Although it should never be a substitute for a face-to-face meeting, if your business and the candidate aren't right for each other it's easier to terminate the process after a 15-minute phone call than during a 1 hour interview in person.

4. There are lots of clever profiling and psychometric profiling tools available on the market today. Some are helpful and insightful in building a team, but others are a costly exercise. Used correctly, they can add real value

to the process, but do your research and be clear on the results you want.

5. Watch out for unconscious bias! It can easily sneak into your decision-making without you realising, impacting the diversity of your team.

CHAPTER 10

The first interview was booked for a little over 48 hours after Dan was due to meet with Anna to put the process together, and understandably Dan was a little apprehensive about whether they could pull it together in time.

As always, Anna was on time, and made a beeline for him as soon as she clocked their table.

"Anna hi - good work trip?"

"Yes, thanks. Productive as always, but glad to be back on home soil. How has your week been?"

Dan raised his eyebrows. "Absolutely crazy - it really has been all hands to the pump to get us moving and in a position where we're ready to interview candidates and the team have pulled so hard to bring everything together so I think we're there."

"Excellent, good work. Tell me where you've got to?"

Dan put his cup down.

- "We screened all the CVs using a scorecard, which worked well.

- Overall, our initial judgements about each CV were on the money, but to see it validated using a scoring system was powerful.

- Once we'd completed the scoring, the next round was our telephone interview. We created a generic script as you suggested, and each respective hiring manager worked through it with each prospective candidate and I think they found it enlightening. If they had to do it all the time, I'm not sure they'd feel as positive but for the first few rounds of interviews it worked extremely well.

- Then we booked the shortlisted candidates into face-to-face interviews with us, and the first one is in about . . ." he looked at his watch, "forty-seven hours and thirty minutes."

Anna laughed. "Wow, you really have been busy. I'm delighted to hear about the telephone interviews. They work on so many levels, from giving you confidence internally that you are making the right decision, to building an early relationship with the candidate and not wasting your time on those that are no longer interested or who applied to tick a box. So, I guess we'd better get cracking on putting this interview process together."

Dan grinned. "I'd say so!"

STEP 10 - THE INTERVIEW PROCESS

"First things first: did you email the candidates to confirm the interview, and will they receive a reminder or a nudge closer to the date and time to jog their memory?" Anna asked.

"We did indeed," Dan answered smugly. "They received an email confirming all the details of the interview as soon as it was booked, and we've scheduled another message for 24 hours before the interview to check they have everything they need and that they are still planning on attending."

"Perfect. It won't completely mitigate any no-shows or last minute dropouts but you've done everything you can to remind them and give them an opportunity to let you know if anything has changed at their end. When we get to building systems and making the processes stick, we could consider adding an automatic text message reminder, as not everyone checks their emails regularly these days."

"Great idea. I'm sure that's fairly simple and in the interim we can look at sending a text message manually to see whether that works." He moved his laptop screen so Anna could see it.

"This is where we're up to. Sarah has dug out some work we've done previously on interviews, questions we've used and so on, but it's all a bit ropy. I don't think ever formalised anything. Usually the team member conducting the interview has a bit of a chat about their CV and experience, and we make the decision from there."

"Right. In your opinion what works and what doesn't work about that approach?"

Dan thought for a moment. "I like that it's informal and helps the candidates feel at ease because that's how we operate. It gives them a chance to be more relaxed and we can understand whether or not we have a connection."

Anna winced slightly.

"Is it the connection thing?" Dan asked

"Yes, 'connection' is like gut feeling. What you're basically saying is you're deciding whether you *like* that person, based on a first impression in an interview. An awful lot of that can be swayed by unconscious bias." She considered her next words carefully. "Say a particular candidate grew up in your hometown. Chances are you'll feel a connection with them and want to like them, regardless of their fit for the position. And let's face it, where they grew up is completely inconsequential to their suitability for a role."

"I get what you're saying, but surely we have to like people to want to hire them?"

"Oh absolutely, but you still have to wade through your personal preferences and unconscious bias to establish whether they are a match for the role and a fit for the company. That's why it's crucial to establish your culture, the traits, the drivers, and the type of person that fits in at your company, because then you can ask yourselves two questions:

- Do they have the skills, qualifications and experience to do the job?

- Will they fit in here?

Dan considered her point. "And how do you establish 'fit', without considering whether we like them?"

"I suggest you base your culture fit on traits, motivators or drivers. Think about the team you currently have: what works well about them in the business you're trying to build? Generally, most business owners will want candidates who are hardworking, passionate about what they do, able to solve problems and good collaborators. I'm guessing most of that will apply to you, but think about anything else that might be specific to Trolley Deals UK. That's how you start to build a strong, clear company culture and you'll then easily be able to identify who will fit, without relying on personal preferences."

"But ultimately, some personal preferences will be built into my company culture, right?" Dan asked.

"Some might creep in, yes, because the business is your baby, after all. But just growing up in your home town or going to the same college or university as you doesn't mean someone is a fit for the culture of the business, even if you sit in the interview with them and personally identify with them. Remember you did a piece of work earlier to create a target persona for marketing efforts? I suggest you revisit that and establish how close that is to defining your culture and the traits and motivators you are looking for in prospective candidates."

"We can do that - we got really clear on who that was so it should be straightforward to distil that into a company culture overview for recruitment purposes."

"Great. The next step is to pull together the structure of the interview. I would suggest that you break it down into two groups:

- Administrative, operational and entry level roles (Group 1).

- Management, leadership, and specialist roles (Group 2).

"That makes sense. The first round of recruits is all in the first category, as we made the decision to hire from the bottom up, restructure most of the middle and then revisit the top."

"Great -that makes the immediate task easier, but let's plan for both," Anna suggested. "Let's talk about Group 1 first.

STRUCTURING THE INTERVIEW PROCESS - GROUP 1

"So, the generic interview script. This is where the traits and drivers come in useful because we can use those to base our questions around. As with all elements of the recruitment process you start by asking why: why are we asking this question and what do we want to know?" She paused for Dan to make notes. "The two biggest mistakes I see interviewers making are either not being prepared and just having a nice chat, or trying to be too clever and asking ridiculous questions, like:

If you were asked to unload a 747 full of jellybeans, what would you do?"

Dan smothered a chuckle. "I'd actually be quite interested to hear what a candidate had to say in response to that."

Anna took a deep breath. "I've seen these scenarios play out and it's clever in theory - you're looking for problem solving, how they would react in an unknown scenario and all that - but all that happens is either the candidate panics, starts sweating and stuttering and you throw them off their game, or if they're more confident, they'll look at you like you're a bit odd and begin to wonder why they are there. It throws off the balance of the interview and, quite frankly, makes the person asking the question look foolish."

Dan could totally see her points. "I'm with you: no silly questions. But how do we avoid the trap of asking the generic questions everyone else asks, just for the sake of it? 'Where do you see yourself in five years' time' and all that rubbish?"

Anna looked quizzical. "Out of interest, why do you think that's a rubbish question?"

Dan thought for a moment. "Now you ask, I'm not too sure. I suppose I think everyone will automatically jump to spouting about how they'd like to be working as one of your top managers etc, but not really mean it. They've fabricated it for the purposes of the interview?"

Anna considered his point and shrugged her shoulders. "Those questions do get a bad rep, and understandably so when they're asked without a purpose. You have to keep remembering to ask yourself why you're asking a question and what result are you hoping for. If this role is a progressive one and you are looking for a future leader in the business, then that's a valid question, but needs to be followed up with, 'And how do you intend to develop the knowledge and skills to get to that position?" or something along those lines, to test how well thought-out the response is. The answer might surprise you."

Dan nodded. "Makes more sense than asking about jellybeans and planes."

"Precisely." Anna continued. "So, my suggestion is that we build an interview question bank."

"A question bank?"

"Broadly, you collate a list of questions grouped into relevant categories, and pull them together into a question bank to form the bulk of your interview. I'll talk you through how to create the question bank, and then I'll walk you through how to structure the face-to-face interview:

- To pull together the question bank, start with your categories, such as 'attention to detail', 'creativity', 'teamwork' and any other category you think is relevant to the Group One roles in your business, and the culture fit of the team. You can have as many or as few categories as you like, so long as you know why they're there and they are relevant to the ultimate success of that person in the role.

- Once you have your categories, build competency-based questions that can help you answer whether that person is a good fit. For example, if the candidate needs to be a strong team player, under the teamwork category the questions could be:

'Tell me about a time you collaborated well within a small team on a specific project?'

'What role have you previously played in team situations?'

- Avoid 'yes and no' questions, like:

'Did you enjoy the subject you studied at university?'

Instead try:

'Why did you choose to study (x) subject at university? Or 'What was the most valuable insight you gained from studying (x) subject at university?

- Avoid asking about hypothetical scenarios and stick to situation-based questions. So instead of,

'How would you react if you uncovered an error in yours or a colleagues' work?'

ask,

'Tell us about a time you have found a mistake in yours or you're your colleagues' work. How did you react?'

- Include a section for the hiring manager to add their own questions about the technical competencies required for the role. This should be completed by the hiring manager or the technical expert in the subject leading the interview. For example, for a Marketing Assistant interview you might like to ask:

'Tell us about how you use a CMS (content management system) in your current role.'

You wouldn't want to ask that of all candidates, so providing a short blank section in the middle of the interview for the hiring manager to complete allows you to tailor the interview, without having to reinvent the wheel each time.

- Include icebreakers and closing questions to give this section of the interview a start, middle and end. Icebreakers should be simple, positive questions to ease the candidate into the interview and help stifle any nerves. Examples of icebreakers include:

'How have you found the recruitment process with us so far?'

'Tell me what you enjoy most in your current role?'

- Closing questions are to wrap up the interview and provide a great opportunity to ask any final questions of the candidate, focused on the role itself instead of personal traits. Where we have already asked about salary and notice period in the telephone interview, this doesn't need to be included at this stage, unless you'd like to sense-check the information from that conversation. Examples of closing questions include:

'Now you've found out more about us as a business, is there anything that has surprised you?'

'Based on what you know, how would you describe our company culture?'

Dan was furiously scribbling notes, desperately trying to take everything in. "Right, I'm up to date with all of that. How about the structure of the interview?"

Anna continued

- Start by greeting the candidate when they arrive and make them feel at ease. Ensure that whoever is responsible for greeting guests is expecting them and makes them feel welcome.

- Have a glass of water ready for them in the room - I usually recommend steering clear of offering tea or coffee, both for their own good and so as not to slow down the start of the interview, and water is better when the nerves kick in. Candidates won't always feel confident enough to ask for or take a glass when offered and end up subtly coughing and regretting their decision. Interviews involve a lot of talking and a glass of fresh water waiting on the table will be gratefully received.

- Introduce everyone present in the room and if it isn't immediately obvious, explain why they are participating in the interview.

- Once pleasantries have been exchanged and introductions have been made, set out the structure of the interview and start by asking them to give you a *brief* overview of their CV. If any of the interviewers have questions about gaps or experience in specific roles they can 'chip in' at appropriate moments to ask. Once the CV overview has been completed you can move into the question bank.

- Always open with at least 2-3 icebreakers.

- Continue to select 2-3 questions from each category, depending on the relevance of each category to the role and the previous questions answered. Often a candidate will go off on a tangent and answer a question before you've asked it, so it's important to actively listen, choose relevant questions and receive the responses you are looking for.

- Finally, select one or two of the closing questions to round off each section of the interview.

- End the interview by asking your fellow interviewers if they have any further questions, and finally asking the candidate whether they have any questions for you.

- Outline the next steps for the candidate before they leave. When will they hear from you? What happens next?"

Anna finished, took a sip of her drink and waited for Dan to complete his note-taking. He finished writing at last. "So much good information there. OK, I have a few questions."

Anna nodded. "Of course, fire away."

"How do we decide who will ask what?"

"Good question, easily solved by designating a lead to the interview - either the hiring manager or your internal recruiter if you have one. That person takes the lead on the interview, keeps an eye on timings and ensures the interview doesn't stall. You then decide between you all who will take the lead on asking the technical specific questions. You'll need to watch out for each other's cues, listen and avoid talking over one another, but you'll find that most groups slip into a rhythm quite quickly."

"And how about timings?"

"I would say to aim for a one-hour interview, with a fifteen-minute spill-over time, so from a diary perspective you'd block out one hour and fifteen minutes per interview. This breaks into:

- 15 minutes for the CV overview

- 35 minutes for the interview question bank

- 10 minutes for the closing question, and their questions

- 15 extra minutes in case any sections run over, and a brief comfort break for the interview panel before the next interviewee arrives.

"Sounds good. How many people and who should be in each interview?"

"In my experience, two is my magic number. One isn't enough to make a fair decision, and three or more could be intimidating to the candidate. If you have the resources it would ideally be a member of your internal recruitment or HR staff, alongside the hiring manager or person responsible for managing or leading the role being hired for. The HR or recruitment staff member would lead the interview, assess for culture fit and keep things on track. The hiring manager is there to listen intently, ask specific questions about the role and make the assessment as to whether the person could perform the role from a technical perspective.

Dana finished writing this all down. "Last few questions: how do we actually decide whether a person is right for the role, and is there another interview?"

"Oh, at *this* level I wouldn't expect to see a second interview unless absolutely necessary. Generally, if you haven't seen everything you need to see by the end of the first stage interview for Group One, something has gone wrong in the process."

"That's interesting; we usually have two interviews as standard, sometimes even three, for all of our roles, but I haven't segregated them into seniority or speciality groups before, and there always seems to be an unanswered question afterwards, or someone else who wants to meet the candidate."

Anna nodded. "It's a really easy trap to fall into: decision by committee. If you have the right process and the right tools to make a decision, you don't need everyone in the business to have an opinion too. It's not efficient and it certainly doesn't provide the right experience for your candidates."

"Understood. So, how do we decide who to hire after the interview?"

"Two tools," Anna explained. "The first, you'll be familiar

with by now: a scorecard. The second is the interview wash-up process. Let's first talk about the scorecard.

- Create a chart on your page with evenly sized boxes, 10 down and 10 across. The column on the far left of the page should be numbered 1- 10.

- Add a 'key' at the top or bottom of the chart in a visible position, explaining that 1 = poor demonstration and 10 = outstanding.

- Pick the top 10 elements from the job description and person specification and put them into the boxes at the top of your chart.

- Each interviewer should review their scorecard prior to the interview, along with all their other interview documentation, such as CVs and the interview question bank. Once reviewed, the scorecard should not be bought into the interview but the interviewers should make notes, being mindful that any notes they make should only be notes that they would be happy to share with the candidate if requested.

- After the interviews, both interviewers should separately complete their scorecards for each candidate, ready for the interview wash-up meeting.

He considered this information carefully. "And what's the interview wash-up?"

"It's by far one of the easiest ways to get a quick, fair and collaborative decision following an interview process. There is nothing worse for all parties involved than when a decision is lingering around for far too long! Here is how it works:"

Interview De-brief (or wash-up) meeting agenda

To be attended by:

Each member of the team who was present for the face-to-face interview.

The key 'Decision Maker' for the role should chair the de-brief meeting. This will usually be the line manager for the role or the technical expert for the department the candidate would be joining.

Timeframe for execution: Within 24 hours of the final candidate interview.

Time allocated to meeting: Between 15 and 30 minutes.

Purpose: To make a unanimous decision, based on the evidence gathered, of which candidate was the best fit for the role.

Pre-preparation required: Scores from the interview scorecard should be tallied by everyone, and each is responsible for bringing their own appropriate notes and documents to the meeting. Everyone will also ideally come with their decision, having not discussed this with other members of the panel prior.

Notes: To facilitate busy teams, any member of the panel can join the meeting via conference voice or video call, should they be unable to be present in person.

Process:

1. First impression vote. Everyone in the group provides a 'yes' or a 'no' in turn, without discussion, based on their evidence and opinion as to the suitability of each candidate. This vote doesn't decide the fate of the candidate, and the

chair notes down all votes for each candidate.

2. The chair moves around the group individually, and each member of the panel gives a summary of each candidate in turn:

   a. Their overall score.

   b. High points of the interview

   c. Low points of the interview

   d. A summary of why the candidate should/should not be appointed.

This information is given without interruption from other panel members, and the chair makes notes for each candidate. When each panel member is finished with their debrief, should a consensus not be reached, a debate should ensue.

The chair remains responsible for all note-taking, and will ultimately have the casting 'vote' in the instance of a 50/50 split.

Once a decision has been reached as to who is the successful candidate, a decision will also be made on:

- Salary

- Proposed start date

This is all passed as confirmation to the recruitment team or line manager to make the offer to the candidate."

Dan whistled, and Anna smiled. "I can send you an email with some templates, overviews and scripts if that'd be helpful?"

Dan looked relived. "Yes please, that would be *great*, thank you. Would have been even better if you'd told me about half an hour ago though!" he laughed, looking at his pages of notes.

"Well, you didn't ask. Anyway - does it all make sense?"

"It's a lot of information, but I'm sure once I start getting to grips with it, it will make things much more straightforward and speed up the process. I'm already starting to see how we can make these decisions without relying on gut feeling, and there are some concrete methods in here to getting this process right."

"Yep, absolutely. Right we need to move onto the changes we make in the process for Group Two interviewees: our specialist, leadership and management roles. Much of the structure remains the same - but let me outline what we keep and what we add."

STRUCTURING THE INTERVIEW PROCESS - GROUP 2

"First things first, we keep the generic interview script, but look at higher level and more specific category questions. One will likely be around management or leadership style so for example:

'Can you tell me about a time you demonstrated strong leadership skills? Describe the situation and the outcome?'

You can expand the question further to ask them what the impact was on the organisation, or whether whatever it was they implemented is still in place today. With leadership positions especially, you're going to be looking for the impact they had on the people in the business, how that candidate inspired their teams, what their leadership style is like, and so on. Secondly, you want to focus on the bottom line: the commercial aspects they bought to the business. What are they like with numbers, and do they have commercial acumen? Consider questions like:

'Tell me about a time you used financial data to support a successful project?'

Next, for your people managers, the most important skill is winning the hearts and minds of others, supporting and encouraging their team to create the best results for themselves and the business, so you could consider something like:

'Tell me about a time you handled conflict between team members?'

Finally, there are your specialists. The preparation for this lies with the hiring manager, or person responsible for line managing this role. As with the Group One interviews you will have an open section for the hiring manager to complete. This is their opportunity to really dig into the candidate's knowledge, understanding and expertise, and if this is a big hire for the business don't be afraid to push a little harder than you might do in interviews for similar positions at a lower level. Each question will be specific to the role and the level you're hiring for."

"Got it," Dan said. "So exactly like the group one interviews but more specific and detailed. Is there any reason why we couldn't build a generic interview script for both the leadership and management interviews?"

"No, none at all."

Dan nodded and continued to make notes, and Anna continued.

"In terms of the structure of the interview, I suggest the first interview stays the same, as does the wash-up and the scorecard, but I would consider adding a second stage interview for the Group Two hires. The likelihood is that these are expensive and crucial additions to the business so it's important to get it right. But it's essential to keep asking the 'why' question. Why are we asking these questions? Why are we asking the candidate to do (x)? Basically, you treat these interviews with more intensity. Friendly intensity, but the stakes are higher so that must be acknowledged."

Dan made a note. "What about second stage interviews?"

Anna thought for a moment. "Well, you said before that it's not unusual for candidates to interview with you multiple times? What do you usually get them to do in the second and third interviews?"

Dan shuffled in his seat. "I'll be honest, I'm not always there and it's often not me running the interviews or making the decisions - I leave that to my team because I can't get involved with everything, but my understanding is that it's often to do with schedule clashes internally and the team will feel it's appropriate to bring the candidate in again to meet with other members of the team who couldn't attend the prior interviews."

"So the candidate is potentially doing the same interview two or three times, with different people, and being asked the same questions?" Anna asked.

Dan looked uncomfortable. "Very possibly."

"Well, luckily that's in the past now. Let's look at how we could run the second stage interviews where they are necessary.

Once you're confident you've answered the 'why are we seeing this candidate again' question, ensure the candidate is aware as early as possible in the process that there will be a second stage interview. There is nothing worse for a candidate than only finding out at the end of the first interview that there will be another hoop to jump through.

Plan intensively for what that second stage will be. How will it differ from the first interview? What is the structure? Who will be present? What are you measuring for?

Rather than simply being a second round of questions and

answers, use this opportunity to create a practical and relevant task for the candidate. Avoid presentations unless it's a sales or commercial role where presentations would be a part of their job.

For example, if you were interviewing a senior finance candidate you could present them with a fictional profit and loss account, cashflow forecast and other financial reporting documents. Give them an allotted amount of time alone with the documents and ask them to discuss their observations on the account, and what advice or comments they would give to the business based on the information they have been given, to simulate them providing a report that would be delivered at a board or Directors meeting.

Ensure the candidate is provided with enough detail for the second-round interview and can arrive with anything they need, but not so much information that there's nothing left to test them with in the interview itself. The purpose is twofold: to ensure they feel comfortable and have an opportunity to shine, and for you to measure whether they would be able to perform tasks in the real world of your business, potentially under pressure and up against deadlines.

- Close the interview with any remaining questions, which should either be pre prepared, or are questions arising from the activity. Allow the candidate time to ask you any final questions as well.

And as per the initial interview, let the candidate know what will happen next and when they are likely to hear from you. Internally you need to arrange and hold a debrief meeting, and a decision should arise as to who to appoint."

Dan sat back in his chair. "That makes so much sense. We've toyed around with making the interviews more dynamic in the past, but we often end up asking candidates to do a presentation on a topic related to their role. I can see how to some candidates, especially our developers and delivery team, that could be intimidating, and we do have candidates who drop out during the interview process - so this certainly feels like it's shining a light on why that might happen."

Anna nodded. "It's a crucial part of the process and if it drags on too long it becomes too time-intensive from the candidate's perspective: it requires them to do lots of work and jump through hoops when they don't even know if they've got the job. You'll either lose them or they'll likely take whatever other job they're being offered at the time."

"We've certainly experienced that over the last few years."

Anna took a sip of her drink and checked her watch. "We're really pushed for time now, but one last thing, which relates to both groups, but more so to Group Two: the offer and negotiation process."

"We get an awful lot of salary negotiations and counter offers, so we definitely need some structure in place to manage this stage of the process better."

"I'll keep it brief for now, and you can follow up with me on email if you've got any questions:

- Aim to make the offer within 48 hours of the candidate's last interview, earlier if possible and always do it by telephone or video call, never email. A telephone call is a much more personal way of delivering a potentially life changing piece of news, and you can gauge the candidates' reaction, and address any concerns or questions they have before accepting your offer.

- Prepare your offer ahead of time. The easiest way to

avoid a negotiation is to offer what is fair. If you've done your housekeeping checks earlier in the telephone interview you should already know what the candidate's salary expectations are and, if they were more than you were willing to pay, hopefully you've managed those expectations. Avoid suddenly trying to low-ball the candidate at this stage. It won't go down well.

- If you are prepared to negotiate, go into the conversation clear on how far you are willing to go and think about other ways you could compromise. Could you offer more flexibility on working hours or more holiday? What else could be of value to the candidate that wouldn't cost you more money?

- Make your offer and let them know you are happy if they'd like to think about it. If they accept immediately, great. If they decide to take some time to think, ask them when they would like you to call back.

- If they ask for a call-back, make sure to ask them if they have any reservations about joining your business, or any further questions. There might be something you can answer at this stage to reassure them and move the conversation on a step.

- Call back when you say you will. If they accept, all well and good. If they negotiate, be ready with your numbers and your alternative offers. If they reject you, ask them for feedback, check they're confident with their decision and simply say thank you very much and wish them good luck.

Dan smiled at the last point. "It's hard not to be bitter sometimes."

"Oh it absolutely is, but recruitment is about long term relationship building, and sometimes the path to finding and building great teams isn't linear. That candidate might crop up again at some point in your business journey when the timing is perfect for both of you, and you'll have maintained a good relationship and your reputation at the same time." She looked at her watch again. "A brief recap on next steps and homework for you:

DAN'S HOMEWORK - STEP 10

- Create your interview question banks. One for Group One, and one for Group Two. Use an online search engine to help find inspiration for the types of questions you can ask within each category.

- Create your interview scorecards - use a similar structure to the ones you've created previously.

- Educate the team on the importance of the post-interview debrief.

- Stop inviting anyone and everyone in your team to interviews decided by committee. Ideally, have two relevant members of staff in the room at any one time, and a second interview is only held for Group Two, and when you know why you want to see them again.

She started collecting up her papers and laptop. "I must dash. It was a huge session today though; I hope you've got everything you need, good luck with the first round of interviews, and you know where I am if you need me. I'll send you over some notes ASAP, which I think will help."

She gave him a brief wave and disappeared. There was so much to take in and they had such a tight turnaround for the first round of interviews, Dan's brain felt like it was on fire. But, armed with this clear structure, he was confident Sarah and her team could do the research to put together everything they needed to get them through.

He went straight back to the office, aware of the tight timeframe they had to put this interview together and aware that Sarah, Tom and Lydia were primed and awaiting instruction to get the process in motion. Exactly as he thought, Sarah was waiting at his desk.

"Ready to go?" Dan asked?

Sarah nodded, primed to take notes as usual.

Dan took a deep breath. "OK, so, Anna will send me some notes on how to structure the interviews and I'll forward them straight to you, but in the meantime let's make a start."

They went through to the meeting room, discussed in detail everything Anna had just advised him, and made a start on the question bank for Group One.

WHAT DAN DID - STEP 10

"Now, what categories do we think should be included in this first question bank?"

After much deliberation they decided on:

- Teamwork

- Problem solving

- Creativity

- Motivation

- Culture/Team fit

- Time Management

These would fit in between the ice-breaker and closing

questions.

Dan looked at the list. "I'm happy with that as a first try. Let's test it, see how well it works and decide what needs to change."

"Agreed," said Sarah. "How did Anna suggest we find questions that would sit within those categories?"

"She said you should find plenty of inspiration online"

"Leave that with me, then. In terms of the interview, shall I put together an agenda for the day and add the structure of the interview, almost like a script that the interviewers will refer to?"

"Great idea. Remember the interviewers will also have to add their role-specific questions. Can I leave that with you to discuss with them and put together?"

"Of course, I've still got Tom and Lydia on this project. I'm confident we can have this done by the end of today."

"Excellent, I'll leave you to it."

Sarah smiled and disappeared to debrief her team and round up the hiring managers to play their part. Dan wondered what he would ever do without her.

5 Key Takeaways From Step 10

1. Wherever possible, segment interviewees into two groups:

    a. Group One - entry level, administrative and operational staff who have no direct reports or leadership responsibilities.

    b. Group Two - management, leadership and specialist experts.

2. Build a set of interview question banks, with specific

categories related to the culture of the business and with a section for technical and role-based competencies built in.

3. Structure your interviews and plan for post-interview debriefs to keep momentum and ensure you don't lose candidates due to a lack of timely feedback.

4. Only call for a second interview for Group Two candidates, and if you are sure about why you are calling them back.

5. When offering a candidate the job, offer them a salary they are worth, and don't surprise them with a last-minute low-ball offer.

The interviews took place over the days that followed and although Dan didn't need to sit in on any of them, as it was the first time the new process was being tested, he debriefed the hiring managers after every couple of interviews to see how effective their new systems were, and he was astounded at the results.

Megan in accounts had been raving about the efficiency and consistency of their new methods and Alex in marketing was over the moon at how painless the interview itself had been. For all jobs in the first round of the process the respective hiring managers made offers to candidates they were excited about - and every single offer was accepted without hesitation. This new strategy was working very well already.

6. "I guess I would expect less negotiation with Group One interviews," Dan told Megan after she updated him on yet another successful hire, "but it's still fantastic news. I'm so pleased you're all happy."

7. He emailed Sarah asking her to send a written offer to all the candidates who accepted, ASAP, and suggested she

draft a standard template for each hiring manager to fill in their specifics, put them into a PDF and send this directly to the candidate from them, cc'ing Sarah in they would have copies centrally, today if possible.

8. He allowed a smile to creep over his face. They really had pulled it off.

CHAPTER 11

As Dan made his way to his weekly meeting with Anna, he couldn't believe how far they had come in a little under three months. The new hires all had written confirmation of their appointments and most of them would be starting within the month.

Once they were trained, phase two of the plan could begin: his internal staff could start migrating into their new roles and do any training they needed, secure in the knowledge that the new round of recruits would keep their previous responsibilities ticking over.

Then it would be on to phase three, assessing gaps remaining in the business in his top tier of management, or specialist roles they were outsourcing and which could probably be undertaken in-house. These were his Group Two interviews, which would complete the next stage of his organisational structure. From there, they'd likely still be making consistent hires, but the hard work would be done, the processes finalised, and they'd finally have a recruitment system that worked.

Anna was at the café before him. She smiled as he joined her. "So - how has your week been? Busy I suspect?"

Dan laughed. "Our offices have been like Piccadilly circus

with all the interviews that have been taking place, but it's been brilliant. Everything went like clockwork: the team loved the new interview structure, and the best part is that it delivered the results we needed. For every single role we now have a new hire that we're excited about, and all of them accepted our offer first time. No negotiation required!"

Anna clapped her hands together in delight. "What a result Dan. So over the next few weeks, you'll have a whole new team joining you. That's exciting, well done. What is the plan with them from here?"

"Well, they have their offer in writing and they'll have their contract on the first day. That's about it, really."

Anna raised an eyebrow. "Do you want the good news or the bad news?"

"Oh. I'll take the good first, please."

"The good news is that you've done an incredible job to get this far and I'm delighted you've sent them an offer in writing and have already settled on starting dates."

Dan grimaced. "And the bad news?"

"You aren't out of the woods yet. We're 90% there, but between being offered the job and starting an awful lot could happen. The candidate could be counter-offered by their current employer, they might have also been interviewing with other businesses and get a better offer, or they could just get cold feet and have a complete change of heart."

Dan was shaking his head. "It just doesn't stop does it?"

Anna laughed. "No, not for a second. With people comes free will and unpredictability, but while you can't stop anyone changing their mind or stop your employees from leaving your business, you can mitigate risk and be confident that you have done everything in your power to influence the final result."

"So, what should we do?"

"Build a keep in touch (KIT) schedule and an on-boarding plan to make sure they arrive on day one and make it past the first week."

STEP 11 - MAKING SURE THE CANDIDATE TURNS UP ON DAY ONE (KIT SCHEDULE) AND ON-BOARDING

- Begin at their start date and work backwards to the present day. I suggest you map it out week to week.

- Create a contact schedule for light-level contact from the appropriate team in the lead up to their first day in the offices. Nothing too full-on, but enough that the new employee remains engaged in the process.

- There are lots of ideas you can build into your schedule such as:

  ◇ Send a card or a personal email to say you're looking forward to them joining the team.

  ◇ Invite them to the offices to meet the team ahead of their first day - perhaps for breakfast or a cuppa at the end of the day so it doesn't interfere with their current working hours

  ◇ Send them a care package with branded merchandise or treats and a handwritten note from their manager.

  ◇ Invite them to a team lunch or event ahead of their first day.

  ◇ Give them early access to an email inbox and copy

them into relevant correspondences so they can hit the ground running.

◇ Ensure they know where they should go on their first day, when and what time.

Dan was writing bullet points of everything Anna said.

"Once you've decided on your activities for each candidate, the hiring manager should plot them into a spreadsheet or table, and share with their team so there are no surprises. The key thing here is communication, ensuring the candidate knows you are excited for them to join the business. There's nothing worse than rocking up on day one with no equipment and feeling like no-one remembered you were coming."

Dan sipped his coffee. "We can definitely do all of that - in fact, I think it would be a really nice springboard for candidates into the business. If we can bring them under our wing at this early stage, not only will we lower risk of losing our new hires, but they'll start to feel like part of the team from the get-go. Sounds like a win win to me."

Anna continued. "Great, so that's the outward facing, or candidate facing, part of this process. We also need to make sure that the cogs are turning internally. I suggest a standard internal checklist for each new employee, so nothing slips through the cracks and you don't waste half of their first morning on the job just sitting on the phone to IT because their email isn't connected properly. The checklist must be relevant to your needs, but some standard points are:

· Equipment: phone, computer, laptop, stationary. Everything the employee will need to do their job, and make sure they have it on day one.

- Email and IT.

- Desk, space and working area. Map out where they will sit and make it obvious you were expecting them.

- Reference checks. It is personal preference whether you want to take them, but my opinion is that anything you can do to lower risk is a good thing, as long as you accept that many companies won't give you anything more than dates and a job title and it can cost time, chasing people around. But it's a worthwhile exercise if you have the resources.

- Prepare their day one and week one schedule. Outline who they will meet with and when, and keep them busy if possible so they'll be buzzing with new information and energy after that crucial day one on the job.

- Prepare their contract, handbook and any other policies they will need access to. Also, ensure they have received a copy of their job description, either with the offer letter or contract.

She continued.

"As I say, this can all be flexible but what's important is that you document it, and provide all candidates with the same experience as part of their on-boarding."

"On-boarding - I'm always confused as to what that actually means and how long should it last?"

Anna nodded. "The official definition is, 'the process of integrating a new employee into an organisation', so your answer is - it takes as long as it takes to integrate a new employee into an organisation."

Dan smiled. "So basically it's how long is a piece of string."

Anna nodded. "It does leave it open as to what is right for your business, but what is important is that you have something in place, you standardise it and you document it. I see our job in recruitment as doing everything we can to make sure the candidates turn up on day one and we support HR in ensuring they everything they need to hit the ground running."

"All about making the start easy and smooth, I guess."

"Exactly. The earliest part of the new employee journey, as they start to orientate themselves into the business, is the tail end of the recruitment process. Once they arrive it's up to HR and their new team to continue the on-boarding process with internal orientation and training. Some businesses claim it can take two weeks, others say six months. I've even heard sources suggest it can take two years."

"How much do you think is best?"

Anna thought for a moment. "Closer to the six-month mark. My definition of an 'integrated employee' is one who can undertake their duties self-sufficiently and begin to add value to a business in whatever capacity they are employed. If you have a great training programme built-in, plenty of internal support and a strong management team, I believe it can be achieved in six months. But again, it varies with each organisation."

Dan was listening intently. "We don't do much on-boarding now, I have to admit. And we have been guilty of candidates arriving on day one and not having equipment, or their desk not being set up. In the past we've tried to brush it off and suggest it's just part and parcel of working in a high-growth, busy business like ours, but it's not really a good enough excuse is it?"

"Afraid not. And that initial encounter will set the tone for their relationship with you for the foreseeable, so it's crucial to get it right."

"Understood."

Anna continued. "But you can define orientation to be more aligned with introducing and familiarisation of the employee's role, team, and the organisation overall, and that could take anything from two days to two weeks. It's more of an 'introduction' phase."

Dan nodded.

"Your homework from today then:

DANS HOMEWORK - STEP 11

- **Build a keep in touch (KIT) schedule**. Build a standard template or spreadsheet and circulate initial ideas of how to populate it. I suggest you create ideas for the schedule based on a notice period of one, two and three months. Leave it up to each hiring manager how they populate it and encourage them to come up with their own ideas, but be mindful of overwhelming the candidate.

- **Create a checklist** to ensure everything from IT to desk space is prepared ahead of the candidate's arrival.

- **Create an orientation plan**. Focus on day one and week one schedules, and then ensure it is aligned with internal training programmes and existing initiatives.

Essentially, all of this is focused around giving the candidate an incredible first impression, leaving no doubt in their mind that they have made the right decision in coming to work for you."

Dan nodded, making notes, "I can't see any reason why we can't bring this together over the next few days. In fact, we might already have some of this in place - I'll check in with Sarah."

"Great. I believe next week will be our final session. How do you feel about everything so far?"

Dan reflected. "It has been a tough journey, and for me personally, the realisation of how wrong we've been getting it all of these years has been painful, and some of it was through sheer laziness or a resistance to following a process. Following a process and formally putting a system in place has made me realise how much easier we could have been finding recruitment all this time. What was a tedious, laborious task has been simplified and demystified over these past few months and I can't imagine going back to where we were."

Anna smiled. "The reason it has been so successful is because you have committed. This initial stage is always hard: whenever you change processes or add systems into a business it's challenging and time-consuming, but you will now be able to enjoy the fruits of your labour, and if you do bring all of those candidates into your business from this round of recruitment and they're all the superstars you think they are, you will be on your way to building something really special. And the next time you need to hire it won't be anywhere near as painful."

"Thank you, Anna, I really appreciate everything you've done for us. I am curious though: what is there left to learn in this process?"

"Ah, the final step in the process will probably be your favourite. Building systems, how we can use technology, and putting in place measures to make sure these shiny new processes stick."

Dan nodded. "Excellent, I look forward to that." He checked his watch. "As usual Anna, great session, but I have got to disappear back to the office."

"Let me know if you need anything, and I'll see you for our final session next week."

Sarah was already at her computer when Dan arrived back at the office.

"How was your meeting with Anna?"

"Good, thanks - we've got a couple more pieces of work to put together for our new candidates, and I think we're nearly there."

Sarah raised her eyebrows. "I'm confused. If we've found them, interviewed them, offered them the job and confirmed it in writing, what more is there to do?"

Dan cleared his throat. "this is actually one of the most precarious parts of the process, because what's to stop them accepting a counteroffer from their current employer or one of our competitors, or changing their mind completely?"

"Well, I guess nothing?"

"Exactly." Dan pulled his desk chair round to her side. "This is where we build a keep-in-touch schedule and talk about on-boarding or orientation. What do we do currently, after the confirmation letters have gone out?"

"We order their computers, get them set up with IT and hope they arrive when they're supposed to."

"Is there any kind of a checklist, timings, or structure, and who is accountable for all this?"

"No, nothing like that. I'll be honest, sometimes it can be a bit last-minute, with a line manager suddenly remembering a new recruit is arriving and whoever is free in admin orders the equipment and gets it ready. There might have even been one or two occasions where the employee has arrived before the equipment, which has been a little embarrassing." She paused. "In fact, I don't think they still work here."

Dan sighed. "It's not really good enough is it? Making this

initial part of the journey as comfortable and smooth as possible will set the tone for our relationship with them, and hopefully help with our retention as we continue to grow. I'd like to create an initial employee experience that they love so much they tell other people about it, and it becomes a core part of the experience of working for us."

Sarah was nodding. "I'm not really sure why we haven't thought about it in more detail before - I guess, like with everything else, there's always something more pressing on the agenda. So where do we start?"

WHAT DAN DID - STEP 11

Dan explained the concept of the KIT schedule and how they could create a simple table with suggestions attached, and encourage hiring managers to come up with their own suggestions to complement these.

"If anyone comes up with a new suggestion, we could ask them to consider if *they'd* have been willing to consider something like that prior to starting a new job, when they were already working for someone else, as a simple internal sense-check?" Sarah suggested.

"Great idea, let's add that as part of the briefing," Dan replied.

They then discussed on-boarding, and decided to build a simple checklist to be completed before each employee starts in the office.

Sarah looked at the list. "In all honesty, this is basic stuff and I'm happy for this to go straight to someone in admin. It could even be a job for one of our more experienced apprentices?"

"That's fine. As long as someone takes responsibility, I don't mind who does it." Dan agreed.

Next, they talked about wider on-boarding, and Dan explained the definition of being 'integrated' in the business.

"How effective do you think our orientation, on-boarding and training is at the moment?" he asked.

"Honestly, it's not something I have a huge amount of involvement with but from what I know, we don't do much in the way of orientation at all.. I do, however, hear the team raving about some of the external training we provide, and our internal specialists are some of the best in the industry. Up until now it's been one of the only hooks we've used to be able to hire great up and coming talent."

"Good to know. Let's work on putting together an orientation plan."

Sarah and Dan discussed everything important for an employee to know on the first day, including a full tour of the building itself, from break-out areas to fire exits. They decided that new employees would have a scheduled meeting with their line manager on day one to discuss their role and ask any questions, with regular a meeting pattern established from then on.

They would assign them a 'buddy' for lunch and break times so they were never left alone for the first couple of days, and the buddy would be tasked with introducing them to other colleagues in the business, to enable them to build a social circle and become embedded in the company culture.

The new employee would be included in meetings, lunch and learns and be encouraged to get to know colleagues in other departments over a cup of coffee as part of the working day. Within the first fortnight they would be sent on their first training course - external, in-house or virtual - in relation to their role and within their first three months they would have a meeting with Dan, either one-to-one or in a small group.

Dan liked to complete tasks at speed so they decided that ideally employees should be orientated, socialised and comfortable by the end of week one, and well on the way to being on-boarded and integrated by the end of month three.

"Is that realistic?" he asked Sarah.

"I think we'll have to have some wiggle room, as everyone learns and reacts to situations differently but I think it is an excellent target, provided we get all our ducks in a row to facilitate it."

"Excellent. Can I leave this with you to formalise and send to the hiring managers?"

Sarah nodded.

Dan paused for a moment. "Just a thought, but is it worth putting all of this in one place, like some sort of hiring handbook or guide for hiring managers, with all of the templates, scripts and guidance in one place?"

"Great idea," Sarah responded. "Lydia is fantastic at design and can put something together no problem. I'll send it over for approval once it's completed"

Dan gave her the thumbs up and moved his chair back to his own desk.

5 KEY TAKEAWAYS FROM STEP 11

1. If a candidate accepts a job it doesn't mean you're out of the woods yet. You still need to ensure you're keeping them engaged, and are staying in touch. A lot can change between you making the offer and them turning up on day one.

2. Build a keep in touch (KIT) spreadsheet or table to plot out key touchpoints, from the offer being made through to their first day in the office. Consider different options for one, two- or three-months' notice periods but ensure your contact is light touch, no pressure and not overwhelming.

3. Create an internal checklist to make sure you are ready for their arrival. Consider equipment, IT and desk space as examples.

4. Make sure you are ready for them on day one. Prepare a schedule, ensure they are introduced to their team and invited to appropriate meetings. You never get a second chance to make a first impression.

5. Consider your on-boarding plan: how long does it take to integrate an employee into your business, and how will you do it? It could be two weeks, two months, or two years - whatever you feel is right for your business, but make it consistent, document it and track the results.

CHAPTER 12

Anna was optimistic about her final meeting with Dan. Even though she was doing this work with her compliments, having felt gratified to help on the day their paths had crossed a few months ago, Dan had been one of her best students to date and it seemed he was reaping the results. They had managed to restructure the business and hire a small team in a little under three months, and a sneaky check at their online presence, ratings and comments showed that their audience was responding well. Overall, the project had been a huge success.

As she entered the café, she could see Dan ready and waiting with their drinks.

"Dan, are you ready for the final session?"

"As ready as I'll ever be."

"Well, as promised, today we are going to talk about how you can pull all of the information I've given you into a coherent system, and make it stick."

"Excellent." Dan was genuinely looking forward to it. Systems and technology were what he lived for.

Step 12 - Systems, Technology and making the process stick

"I'll start by saying that there is absolutely nothing wrong with running the entire process manually. You have all of the scripts, templates, guidance and structure in place, and candidates can be easily managed through the process with a simple spreadsheet and assigning someone to be accountable for effectively project managing each hire. This keeps everything moving, by having a central point of contact for the different stages of the process."

Dan looked a bit disappointed.

She laughed. "But I understand you can't wait to turn this into something more technical, so let's talk about applicant tracking systems, or ATS for short."

"OK, and an applicant tracking system is?"

"A recruitment system. It's a software application, often online, usually cloud-based, that enables you to manage your recruitment electronically. It can automate and map the whole candidate journey all the way from the initial application, to an offer letter going out and everything in between. Here are some key points about how it works:

- It's a seamless integration with the careers page on your website. Applicants apply for jobs on the front end of the ATS (your careers page) and land in the back end, complete with CV, application form and any other details you've asked them to input at the start.

- You use the ATS to manage candidates through the process - particularly useful if you experience a high volume of applicants. You can build in template emails -

customisable, so it sounds like a human being has written it, as opposed to a faceless robot - and these can be anything from a polite rejection to an interview booking or a job offer.

- You can immediately see all details about a candidate, from when they applied, to what stage they are at now, keeping all your candidate data in one place.

- You can also use the system to arrange interviews. Good ATS systems will send out interview confirmations and follow them up with email or text message reminders to help mitigate any 'no shows' and save time internally by not having to chase candidates manually.

- You can create talent banks, tagging applicants based on their experience and key words in their CV or application. This is a great way to store speculative applicants, or applicants who are great for the business, but you haven't quite found the right role for them yet - the talent pool we discussed earlier. Once you have this, the possibilities are endless.

- Multiple users can communicate within the system, all leaving notes and updates on each candidate in one place without the need for details bouncing around internally via email. In addition, you can have different 'levels' of users to ensure that certain users can only see data related to their vacancy, not all of the candidates and information stored in the system.

- Most good systems are compliant with up-to-date data regulations, and candidates will confirm to the T&Cs of you storing their personal data, your privacy policy and understand how they can remove their data from your system. As long as you act within those guidelines it gives you the protection you need to store personal data.

You *can* also look at functions like automatic screening when a candidate applies, based on keywords and phrases it scans for from the candidates' CV and application, but I would encourage you to stay away from that type of system. Focus on one that's is customisable and delivers a great candidate experience. There is nothing like the human touch when it comes to screening CVs and I'm not a big believer in 'bots' or overdoing technology when it comes to recruitment."

Dan was listening intently. "So how do we get one of these in our business?"

"It's a straightforward process:

- Build a requirements list. Think about everything you want the system to do, and how you would like it to do it.

- Map out your recruitment process. How does the process run internally? What scripts or templates will need to be built into the system?

- Map out a candidate journey. How would you like the experience to run from the perspective of the candidate?

- Consider any trigger points. For example, if a certain email needs to go out at a certain time, what action in the system will trigger that email.

- Once you're confident you know what you want from the system, do some research. There are hundreds of companies on the market, some better than others. Pick a handful of companies that offer what you need and set up free trials.

- Once you have undertaken the trials, pick a maximum of three providers and meet them (virtually or in person) to discuss your specific requirements. If you are happy with your shortlist, ask them to put in a proposal.

- Check your proposal carefully. ATS systems will often have a 'set-up and build' charge plus on-going monthly cost, usually on a twelve-month contract at least. Additionally, if there is anything you want your system to do that isn't in the initial brief, you may have to pay extra developer time to add it in later. Be clear that your ATS will do everything you need it to do before you make your final decision.

Dan thought for a moment. "Do you think we could build it ourselves?"

Anna smiled. "Not every business would have the in-house capability to do it but I think you guys could. Why don't you look at how other systems are put together, maybe do a few free trials and see if you think it's viable? You'd be able to create something truly bespoke, not to mention saving quite a lot of money. You just need to be sure that you have the time and resources to pull it together."

"I'm confident we do; I'm thinking of something simple initially, with a view to improving as we go."

"Always the best way."

Dan took a breath. "OK, the million-dollar question now: how do we get all of this to stick? It's all well and good creating these systems and processes, but if no-one uses them, we're back to square one"

"Absolutely. The crucial element with all of this is the buy-in of your team. If they aren't involved or don't believe in what you're doing then it won't stick, so keep them involved every step of the way. Next, you must think about how to simplify. I've encouraged you to create templates and basic scripts, which are evergreen and can be used repeatedly just by making small tweaks to keep them relevant. If your team must constantly re-invent the wheel, they'll quickly lose interest."

"Agreed."

Anna continued. "The ATS we've just spoken about will create a structure and some automation, which will help to embed this as the 'new way'. You can do anything else you need to help ensure employees have all the information they need at their fingertips, so they don't get creative because they can't find the right material."

"We've actually created an internal handbook, which will signpost the hiring managers to the scripts, templates and guidance they need. That, coupled with the ATS, should mean that there are no excuses for not being able to run the process the way it should be run."

"Great idea." Anna took a sip of her drink. "The final step is hiring someone to take total responsibility for your recruitment. It will become their responsibility to ensure *all* of this happens and support the hiring managers through the process. In all honesty, looking at your hiring plans I do think you will need someone to take care of recruitment exclusively for the foreseeable for your business."

Dan thought for a moment. "It's something I've been thinking about a lot. Sarah is almost completely tied up in this recruitment work, and once this is launched and tested I need to step away from working on this day to day, as does she. I am concerned, however, that if we take our focus off this project we'll slip back into our old habits and all of this will have been for nothing. But do we really need to hire someone solely for recruitment?"

Anna smiled, knowingly. "Just have a think about it."

"I will." Dan paused. "So, that was our final session."

"Well, the final session in terms of helping you to pull together your recruitment processes, strategy and systems, yes, but I'm always around if you need me and I think the conference in New York will be a game-changer for you."

"I'm really looking forward to it, but I'm also sorry to see the end of these sessions, despite the amount of extra work it's given me and Sarah these last few months. It's put a real spark back in the business for me, and I feel like we're back on track."

"That's great to hear." Anna raised her cup. "To you and the rest of the team at Trolley Deals UK, for completely transforming your recruitment, being excellent sports and helping your business to grow and transform in the process."

Dan smiled and clinked his coffee cup against hers.

"We're not done yet though: here are your final pieces of homework."

DANS' HOMEWORK - STEP 12

1. Decide what system you will use to manage the process. Is your requirement small enough that you can stick to paper templates and a spreadsheet? Do you need to buy an off the shelf Applicant Tracking System or have something built bespoke? Do you have the in-house capability to build a system yourself?

2. If you decide to build it yourself, assign someone to the project and ensure they have the time and resource to complete it. It will be more cost-effective than doing it yourself.

3. Map out the journey from both sides. What should the workflow look like internally, and how should the

candidates experience it?

4. Create a plan for how the new system and process will 'stick'. How will you embed it into the team and how will you monitor progress? Who will take responsibility for managing the structure and keeping you all on track?

And that," Anna said, closing her laptop. "Is that."

Dan paused, almost feeling sad. "I can't thank you enough Anna for everything you've done for us. You've completely turned things around. If there is ever anything I can do for you, please just say the word."

Anna smiled. "Well, if you know anyone that could benefit from what I do and can make an introduction, I'd be very grateful."

"Of course I will." He clocked the time on his phone. "I've got to head off now Anna, but I'll see you in New York in a few months' time, and we must keep in touch."

"Oh definitely. I'll be keeping tabs on your progress, and you keep me updated with how it's all going."

They said their final goodbyes and Dan left feeling lighter than ever and ready to build a system to pull the whole process together.

When he got back into the office, he headed straight over to the developer team, making a beeline for Neil, one of their lead software developers.

"Neil, have you got a moment - there's a project I'd like to run by you."

"Course Dan, just let me finish this and I'll swing by your desk."

"Perfect - thank you."

Within twenty minutes Neil was there.

"What's the project you have in mind, Dan?"

"I'm sure you're aware of the recruitment project we're currently undertaking - in fact, I think you've been in some of the interviews recently?"

He nodded. "I have - they've been in a different league to where we've been before."

Dan was pleased. "Excellent. We've come to the final stage now and it involves building a piece of recruitment software. Its official name is an 'applicant tracking system', and broadly it sits as an application portal behind our website where we manage applicants through the process automatically."

Neil nodded, understanding the idea straight away. "It's not something I've done before but I can't see any reason why it wouldn't be possible to build something basic to do this. Let me do some research, so I'm clear on what it is. Then, do you think you could put together some high-level specifications for me? What you want it to do, what the workflow looks like - that type of thing?"

"I've got a clear idea so let me pull together some documents for you, and if you could do some research that'd be great. Once we get to that stage, if you can give me a rough idea of how long it might take to pull together at least a sandbox version that we can test, I'd be grateful."

"No problem, leave it with me and I'll come back to you by the end of the week."

"Much appreciated."

Dan caught up with Sarah next.

"How are the KIT schedules coming along?"

"Really well. No major disasters, as far as I can tell our new intake is engaged and raring to go. The first new employee is due in next week and the general consensus amongst the team is that this is working well."

Dan smiled. "Exactly what I wanted to hear."

"I saw in the diary that you had your final session with Anna today - I didn't realise there was still more work to do." Sarah looked apprehensive.

"Yes, I wanted to update you on the last step of the process, have you got a minute?"

She nodded and pulled up a chair.

Dan talked her through his conversation with Anna, the concept of the applicant tracking system, and that Neil was on the case to see how viable building it in-house would be..

Sarah nodded. "What do we need to do to help Neil put something together?"

WHAT DAN DID - STEP 12

"We need to:

- Map out the workflows, from both an internal and external perspective.

- Create the external candidate journey.

- Provide Neil with all our scripts and templates. Documents like the application form and the telephone interview script can then be built into the system.

- Devise a suite of email templates for every step of the process from a rejection email to an interview invitation email, a job offer email and everything in between.

- Decide on any special functions we need or want the system to perform.

I want to be clear that I don't want anything too complex at this stage. I'd rather build something basic, that focuses on automating and streamlining processes at our end and provides an excellent experience for the candidate externally."

"Understood." Sarah thought for a moment. "With all of the work we've done on this already, with all the templates and scripts we already have, I can bring this information together quickly and liaise with Neil to get us to a stage where we can at least test and tweak."

"That would be fantastic. I'll leave it with you, and perhaps just loop me back in when you get to the testing stage?"

"Absolutely - I think we can have something in a matter of weeks."

"Thank you, Sarah." Dan smiled appreciatively. "It's all yours."

Over the next few weeks Sarah and her small team worked with Neil to create the system and map out the workflows. They added candidate text message reminders, crafted well-written emails that sounded as if they had been written by a human being not a robot and built a fully functioning talent pool to start to build their own talent pipelines, using basic keyword and Boolean search strings.

Almost three weeks later, Dan had a link pop into his inbox from Neil.

Dan,

Play away.

Let me know your feedback.

Neil.

It was the link to the new recruitment system. Dan immediately clicked it and was led to a branded homepage with a dashboard to let them know candidate progress, a message centre to flag up any new messages and a to-do list to keep everyone on track. As he navigated the system, he could see all the templates Sarah had built for the various stages of the process, blending in seamlessly with the technology Neil had put behind the system to make it functional. There was a test candidate in the system already, and Dan could immediately see how easy it would be to automate candidates through the process and store their data. He was delighted.

He spent the next hour checking for any errors or changes to be made but everything worked like a dream. He emailed Neil back CC-ing Sarah and Alex.

Neil

Love it! No changes. Can you work with Alex to get the front end of this up on the careers page?

I will announce the change to all staff, and Sarah can you please liaise with all hiring managers to set up a training and cascade session, so everyone is up to date as soon as we can manage it.

Great work guys. We're there.

D

5 Key Takeaways from Step 12

1. Decide how you will manage your system. Spreadsheets and paperwork? An online workflow or project management software, or an online system. Consider your needs and your budget when making your decision.

2. Be clear on what you want the system to do and the style of system that works for your business. Shiny graphics and state-of-the-art, or something more functional?

3. Map out the candidate workflow from both an internal and an external process so you can be clear that it matches the process you have already drawn up.

4. Customise communications wherever possible. Keep the candidate journey engaging and fluid. They will know the messages are automated but don't make it too obvious.

5. Be sure to get buy-in from your team, and cascade user guides and training sessions effectively. There is no bigger waste of investment than a piece of software that no-one uses.

That week, many of the new recruits had joined the team and they were all excellent. The change in the office was palpable, there was an energy that hadn't been there since the early days, and everyone felt this would be their best year yet.

Dan closed his tired eyes at last. They were there. A lot of hard work, sweat and tears had gone into this project, but they had made it. His recruitment finally *worked*.

EPILOGUE

As the thunderous applause began to die down and Anna took to the stage, Dan was taken aback by how packed the conference centre was. To him, she was just Anna who he'd met every week for a couple of months in a coffee shop, but it was clear now that in her world she was a big deal!

She'd been right about how much he would gain from attending the conference he'd already set up drinks meetings with business owners from all over the world, one or two of which had worked with Anna and were keen to swap stories, and he'd attended numerous workshops on recruitment technology and the future of hiring.

His team had almost doubled in the six months since he met Anna and they weren't far off the one hundred staff mark. Space had been a struggle but with some careful planning, scheduling, working from home and hot-desking they were all still just about squeezed in, but an office move was on the cards in the new year. Nigel, his investor, was delighted with the rapid growth of the business and was spending more time in St Tropez and less time on the phone to Dan - for which Dan was grateful.

After the project had completed Dan realised that Sarah was completely underutilised, and quickly made the decision to appoint her as Chief Operations Officer. She was the yin to his yang and was doing an incredible job of managing the day-to-day operations of the business. With him now free to exercise creativity and do the things in the business that the CEO *should* be focusing on, the business was back on its rapid growth trajectory.

The staff he already had at the start of this project were all still going strong, except one notable loss: Lydia. After her stellar performance supporting Sarah through the recruitment project, she had left the company to start her own virtual assistant business. Dan had wanted her to step into Sarah's shoes as his new PA, but how could he prevent her from living her dream? Trolley Deals UK still used her services on an outsourced basis when Sarah or Dan needed her, and Dan's new assistant was learning the ropes quickly, thanks in part to Lydia and Sarah's excellent handover but also to Molly, their outsourced in-house recruiter, and her understanding of his needs and his business to find him the right person.

Unable to justify the overheads of a hiring someone to run the recruitment, Anna had suggested using Molly from her team - and it was the perfect solution. She blended in seamlessly and worked for him as though she was his recruitment team, with occasional support from Anna, but he didn't need to employ her: she worked for him on a flexible basis, just like Lydia now did. The outsourcing model, coupled with an effective talent planning and recruitment structure, worked well.

Anna received a standing ovation, and rightly so. She invited all attendees to take a copy of her new book as they left - a read Dan was looking forward to getting stuck into.

Dan and Anna had made plans to meet for a drink with both Emily and Anna's husband, Mike. Emily arrived first, laden with bags, and joined Dan at the bar.

"You've had a good day I see!" He raised an eyebrow at her haul.

"Naturally," she smiled and signalled to the waiter, a huge diamond ring glittering on her ring finger. "I had to get a whole new wardrobe to match *this*." wiggling her hand in front of his face.

Dan laughed. On their first day in New York he'd taken her for a walk around Central Park, got down on one knee and popped the question. They were now excitedly planning a late summer wedding the following year.

Anna and Mike joined them, and on hearing Dan and Emily's' good news they insisted on ordering a bottle of champagne in celebration.

When the glasses were poured, Dan cleared his throat. "Actually Anna, I'd like to also use this opportunity to thank *you*. Without you, we wouldn't be here and none of this would have been possible." He looked purposefully at Emily's left hand. "You've changed my business and my life and, let's face it, you were a complete inspiration up on that stage. So, thank you, congratulations and long may our friendship continue. To Anna."

"To Anna." They all chorused.

As the evening played out, Dan thought over how they had ended up here and was grateful for that chance meeting. Opening the first few pages of her book, he had a feeling of familiarity wash over him.

"Hey Anna, who's Stan and why does he run a business called ShoppingApp?"

Anna paused and they all started laughing.

"I have no idea what you're talking about."

If you enjoyed this book, please provide me with a rating and some feedback via Amazon. It makes all the hard work worth it.

Are you struggling with recruitment?

Is it beginning to hold back the growth of your business? Do you spend your time in firefighting mode, and never seem to have the right people in the right place at the right time?

It's exhausting. I get it.

To help you out, I've put together a selection of the resources that Anna works through with Dan in this book. Between that and the advice given in the chapters of this book, you'll be well on your way to recruitment (and ultimately business) success.

You can access those resources here:

https://mailchi.mp/27d5a64ae95a/recruitment_resources

ANNEXE

THE TWELVE STEPS TO HIRING SUCCESS

Step 1 - The power of the organisational structure

1. Organisational structure forms the foundations of talent planning, organisational growth and the people plan.

2. Organisation charts provide clarity when they focus on the roles in the business, not specific members of staff.

3. Build the structure with the roles in the business first, slotting appropriate names in as a secondary activity.

4. People will likely have more than one role within the business - some more than five. This is completely normal, provided no team member is under-performing, stretched beyond capacity and is in a role that allows them to work to their full and true potential.

5. The purpose of the organisation chart and structure is to understand where the gaps, stretch and resources are currently deployed. It is NOT a hierarchical snapshot of the company. It is worth researching other methods of organisational structure such as Holacracy, to understand what the right fit for your business is. Sometimes the

traditional way is the simplest, with a view to adjusting as you grow.

Step 2 - Talent Planning and Recruitment Binoculars.

1. Planning and timing are the cornerstones of building a successful, proactive recruitment strategy.

2. Recruitment plans and forecasts must have flexibility built into them. Much like a cash-flow forecast, it's a mix of facts, best-guess and goals. Your predictions will change, and the plan must have the capacity to change with it.

3. It is rarely a surprise that you need to hire. Make a note to regularly pick up your 'recruitment binoculars' to keep on top of the changes happening in your business.

4. Outsourcing, automation and grass-roots hiring, or succession planning, are a key part of your talent planning and recruitment strategy. Use each element appropriately to future-proof your business.

5. Specialist or senior roles can sometimes take six or even twelve months to fill, by the time you've accounted for time to hire and notice periods. Don't let it keep surprising you, and always try to stay out of fire-fighting mode.

Step 3 - Treat your recruitment like marketing: Employer Branding

1. **Define who you are looking for** and really get into the details. Where would they hang out? What types of things do they like and dislike? What are their lifestyle choices? Get really clear on this picture to build your strategy.

2. **Where will you find this person?** Can you access them through social media? Real life events? Specific websites? Industry publications? If you've been clear enough on

who you are looking for, you'll know where to find them.

3. **How will you target them?** Based on where you think you'll find them, build a strategy to engage with them and develop a voice and messaging that will engage them. Is it through a paid-for social media campaign? A blog post in an industry publication? Sponsoring or appearing at an event or conference?

4. **Get to know your competition**. Research and understand how your competitors are positioning their available jobs and decide what you could emulate and what you could do better to build your unique employer brand.

5. **Build your platforms**. A careers page, social media strategy or applying for awards are just some of the ways you can build a 'green light always on' recruitment marketing campaign to consistently attract passive candidates.

Step 4 - An engaged internal talent pool and network building

1. **Talent pools** can be as basic as a spreadsheet and secure folders, or as complex as bespoke software. Find what is right for your business and regularly review it.

2. **Take a view on the content** of your pool approximately every six months. Going back much further than that (unless candidates are pro-actively opting in) rarely yields results.

3. **Look at ways of retaining control** over who sits in your talent pool and how they are categorised. Don't automatically put a 'drop your CV off here' link on your website, for candidates to self-populate. You need to be proactive about filtering and filling the pool with talent that will be valuable to your business. A talent pool is only as useful as the information and content within it.

4. **Don't let the content of your talent pool sit passively.** Engage with it. Develop value-added content, such as tips and blogs alongside vacancy promotion to ensure you are the first business your ideal candidates think of when the time is right.

5. **How can you start to move away from rigid job descriptions for your existing team?** While everyone has a place in the structure of the business, start to build a strategy for developing cross-pollination skills between departments and team members to future-proof your business and increase internal capabilities, building an internal talent marketplace.

Step 5 - Building and Documenting a Recruitment Process

1. A robust process is the key to building a successful recruitment strategy. If you don't have a process to test and measure against, you're reinventing the wheel each time.

2. Use a standardised structure and tailor it to the resources and people you have available.

3. Consistently test and measure your process so you can keep what's working and tweak the stuff that isn't.

4. It will take time and energy upfront to create the processes and structure, but think of it as an evergreen activity: once it's done, the first iteration is completed.

5. Don't lose sight of the fact that it's a live process - keep improving and tweaking to keep it relevant with the changes in your business.

Step 6 - A Job Description Does What It Says On The Tin and Step 7 - Writing a Compelling Job Advert

1. A job description is the internal-facing document, the foundations of the process, and is intended to be straight-talking 'fluff'-free definition of the responsibilities and deliverables of the role.

2. A person specification outlines the skills, experience and attributes of the desired candidate and can be a standalone document or a part of the job description. It is also an internal-facing document.

3. The job advert is the external piece of copy, using the information gathered in the job description and person specification, written in a clear, engaging and candidate-centric format. Think of it as the shop window to your careers offering, written to attract a passive candidate who isn't actively looking but may be tempted if the offer is good enough.

4. Don't mix and match the two documents.

5. Don't simply copy and paste a job description (or any elements of it) and call it an advert.

Step 8 - Creating A Candidate Marketing and Search Strategy

- Always begin a new marketing and search campaign by reviewing your company's overarching target candidate persona and tweaking it to ensure it is relevant to the role.

- Consider what is appropriate for the level and department of the role. Is a junior role suited to a job board search and clever advertising campaign? Is it a senior or specialist role that will require a proactive online search and contact method? One size doesn't fit all.

- What's your budget? Do you need a budget? If you are spending money on advertising, always do your research. Contact the advertising platform directly and ask them for statistics on your target demographic. For example, how many candidates do they have registered in X industry or in X location.

- Have you considered pay-per-click (PPC) advertising for your recruitment? It can be a way of controlling your costs, quickly measuring your return on investment, and specifically targeting the right demographic of candidates.

- If you don't have one in place already, an internal employee referral scheme can be a great way to encourage your current team to think about the people in their networks who could be a great fit for your business. You'd be surprised how far a small monetary reward can go in terms of jogging people's memories.

Step 9 - The Candidate Shortlisting Process

- Decide what tools work best for you and the business to move candidates from simply being names and words on a piece of paper to people in front of you in an interview. Consider a well thought-out, succinct and engaging application form and scorecards to support your decision-making process.

- Scorecards are a great way to justify the decisions you make: they can easily be created in alignment with job descriptions and company culture statements, and tweaked for the varying levels of experience and skillset within each team.

- Always utilise a telephone interview as part of your screening process. Although it should never be a substitute for a face to face meeting, if your business and the candidate aren't right for each other it's easier to terminate the process after a 15 minute phone call than during a 1 hour face to face interview.

- There are lots of clever profiling and psychometric profiling tools available on the market today. Some are helpful and insightful in building a team, but others are a costly exercise. Used correctly, they can add real value to the process, but do your research and be clear on the results you want.

- Watch out for unconscious bias! It can easily sneak into your decision-making without you realising it.

Step 10 - The Interview Process

1. Wherever possible, segment interviewees into two groups:

   a. Group one - entry level, administrative and operational staff who have no direct reports or leadership responsibilities.

   b. Group Two - management, leadership and specialist experts.

2. Build a set of interview question banks, with specific categories related to the culture of the business and with a section for technical and role-based competencies built in.

3. Structure your interviews and plan for post-interview debriefs to keep momentum and ensure you don't lose candidates due to a lack of timely feedback.

4. Only call for a second interview for Group Two candidates, and when you are clear in yourself about why you are calling them back.

5. When offering a candidate the job offer them a salary they are worth and don't surprise them with a last-minute low-ball offer.

Step 11 - Making sure the candidate turns up on day one (KIT Schedule) and on-boarding

1. If a candidate accepts a job it doesn't mean you're out of the woods yet. You still need to **ensure you're keeping them engaged**, and are staying in touch. A lot can change between you making the offer and them turning up on day one.

2. **Build a keep in touch (KIT) spread-sheet** or table to plot out key touch-points from the offer being made through to their first day in the office. Consider different options for one, two- and three-months' notice periods but ensure your contact is pressure-free and not overwhelming for the candidate.

3. **Create an internal checklist** to make sure you are ready for their arrival. Consider equipment such as IT and desk spaces.

4. **Make sure you are ready for them on day one**. Prepare a schedule, ensure they are introduced to their team and invited to appropriate meetings. There is nothing worse than a new employee arriving on day one and it seems as if no-one knew they were coming. You never get a second chance to make a first impression.

5. **Consider your on-boarding plan.** How long does it take to integrate an employee into your business, and how will you do it? It could be two weeks, two months, or two years - whatever you feel is right for your business, but make it consistent, document it and track the results.

Step 12 - Systems, Technology and making the process stick

1. Decide how you will manage your system. Spreadsheets and paperwork? Online workflow or project management software, or an online system? Consider your needs and your budget when making your decision.

2. Be clear on what you want the system to do and the style of system that works for your business. Shiny graphics and state-of-the-art, or something more functional? What is important for your business?

3. Map out the candidate workflow from both an internal and an external process so you can be clear that it matches the process you have already drawn up.

4. Customise communications wherever possible to keep the candidate journey engaging and fluid. They will already know the messages are automated don't make it too obvious.

5. Be sure to get buy-in from your team, and cascade user guides and training sessions effectively. There is no bigger waste of investment than a piece of software that no-one uses.

ABOUT THE AUTHOR

Rosie Skinner is a recruitment expert, speaker and the Founder and Director of Mployable - Talent Strategy and Recruitment on Subscription, also known as the Outsourced In-House Recruitment Team.

She's been in the recruitment industry for over ten years, in recruitment agency roles in her early days, through to in house recruitment and HR managerial roles in the latter part of her career. Rosie is CIPD and REC qualified and has spoken at prestigious industry events such as 'Disrupt HR' and 'Inspire Recruitment' as well as numerous business events and workshops.

Rosie loves recruitment but resents the reputation the industry has.

She believes that 'Done right, and done fairly for both parties, a recruitment professional has the capability to transform a business. It doesn't have to be expensive, or shrouded in questionable T&Cs. Recruitment at its heart is built around people and relationships - so it needs to be focused on a service and an experience - not a transaction.'

Rosie's creation of Mployable is a response to that need for change in the outsourced recruitment industry. It's time for a shake-up, and she's leading the charge.

ABOUT MPLOYABLE

Mployable isn't another recruitment agency.

We offer talent strategy and recruitment on subscription to high-growth scaling businesses. Think of us as your outsourced in-house recruitment team.

We're here to empower businesses to get better at hiring, allowing them to scale and grow successfully.

If you resonated with Dan and want to find out more about how Mployable can transform your business, head to:

www.Mployable.co.uk or say hi via hello@mployable.co.uk

Printed in Great Britain
by Amazon